A Guide to The Presbytery

ANDREW HERRON

THE SAINT ANDREW PRESS
EDINBURGH

First published in 1983 by
THE SAINT ANDREW PRESS
121 George Street, Edinburgh

Copyright © Andrew Herron 1983

ISBN 0 7152 0567 6

Printed and bound in Great Britain by
Thomson Litho Ltd, East Kilbride, Scotland

Contents

Preface

It is six years since, at the instigation of the late Lord Ballantrae, I produced a little booklet designed to act as a guide to the General Assembly—particularly for the first-timer. Such was the welcome accorded to the work that, about three years later, I followed it with a similar booklet intended to assist the ordinary member of a congregation in finding his way through the intricacies of congregational management within our Kirk. From time to time suprise has been expressed that I had not tried to apply a comparable technique of unravelling to the affairs of the Presbytery with which, it has been suggested, I might have been expected to have been intimately familiar, not to say deeply concerned.

I think it has been probably just the extent of my commitment at Presbytery level that has made me unwilling to attempt to write about that court. That restriction being now lifted I am making this third little contribution to the series. I am far enough away from it now to see it all more clearly—or so I hope.

Let me emphasise that this is not meant to be an authoritative text-book on the subject of the Presbytery—those who are looking for that must turn to Cox. It represents rather a kind of personal commentary on the work of the Presbytery. Being involved with Acts and Regulations at the level where you have to apply them and try to make them work gives you an insight denied to the sheer academic legislator. I have felt at liberty to "write dangerously", to indicate what I consider the weaknesses, the inadequacies, the ambiguities, the—dare I say it— occasional stupidities within our system. For all such critical comments (and there are many of them) I, naturally, accept full responsibility. It is my hope that they may give the work a degree of interest it would not otherwise possess. Please feel free not only to disagree with me, but to enjoy doing so. There's no point in being wrong if you don't get some pleasure out of it!

Wherever it has seemed appropriate I have added little historical notes showing how situations have developed, for it seems to me we can usually understand laws best when we see why they came to be enacted. Legislation does not begin in the head of a jurist; it begins with a practical problem for which provision has to be made. Someone once said that law is just common sense. I wouldn't go all the way with that—sometimes it's just uncommon nonsense! But certainly an understanding of the reason behind the law can assist considerably in the wise application of it.

I hope the booklet may prove of interest—and perhaps even value—to Presbytery Clerks and others responsible for the smooth running of their courts, but it is directed in the first place to the "greenhorn", to the newcomer (or at least comparative newcomer) to the Presbytery who wants to be deeply interested and concerned but who feels very much at sea and would like to understand better what it's all about.

Glasgow   ANDREW HERRON
November 1982

1

How It Began

In this world some things happen by design and others by accident, and it is not uncommon for the latter to prove of greater importance than the former. In particular there are institutions whose life began on a drawing-board as part of the carefully designed plan for a larger whole, while there are others that came into being more or less by chance to meet an *ad hoc* situation that emerged as the larger plan was developing and that later came to fill the central place within that whole. It is to this "accidental" class that the Presbytery belongs — which may seem odd considering how very central a place the Presbytery has come to fill within the Presbyterian form of Church government.

Andrew Melville, the architect of Presbyterianism, in his conception of the pyramid of Church rule envisaged a three-tier structure with the General Assembly at its peak, and the Kirk Session at its base, and with, between these two, the Provincial Synod as the effective body in charge of local rule. But as the number of parishes increased the burden upon Synods became relentlessly heavier, and, for considerations of simple geography if for no other, it was a burden too heavy to be borne. So, with a view to easing this burden, recourse was had to a group of bodies that had been in existence since the days of the Reformation and whose purpose had been to provide a forum where ministers and people could meet for the study of the Scriptures. These gatherings were known as "The Exercises" or "The Weekly Exercises". Even after they had been converted into "Presbyteries" and invested with many additional responsibilities they continued to open their proceedings on every occasion with sermon and discussion of Scripture. The "exercise" of that day, reduced in extent and dwarfed in importance, has survived as the "opening devotions" of today's Presbytery meeting.

By the time Melville produced his Second Book of Discipline (adopted by the General Assembly in 1581) he included Presbytery along with Kirk Session, Synod and General Assembly as part of the Presbyterian structure—a new tier of government sandwiched between Session and Synod and destined to take over the bulk of the responsibility originally designed for the latter body. Presbytery had arrived.

It was in 1592 that there was passed what has been described as the Magna Charta of the Kirk wherein King and Parliament acknowledged and ratified Church government by General Assemblies, Synods, Presbyteries, and Kirk Sessions. Presbytery had arrived to stay.

Over the years the wisdom of this step has been abundantly justified so that Presbytery has come to be seen, in the words of the latest edition of Cox, as "the characteristic and in some sense the fundamental court, since, on the one hand, it directly superintends not only Kirk Sessions but the whole ecclesiastical activity within its bounds, and, on the other hand, elects annually those ministers and elders who are to constitute the General Assembly." The extent of the responsibility of the Presbytery has increased enormously of recent years, as is indicated by the fact that Mair in his *Digest of Church Law* published in 1897 was able to dispose of the Powers and Duties of the Presbytery in five pages, whereas the latest edition of Cox (1976) requires thirty-one pages to cover the same subject.

It shall be my aim in the succeeding pages to set forth the constitution, the method of operation, and the business of the present-day Presbytery.

2

Who Are Its Members

The point should be made at the outset that in the minds of those who designed the Presbyterian system there was firmly implanted the principle that every inch of Scotland must be taken into account so that no single inhabitant should be outwith the care of the National Kirk. The whole land was already divided up into parishes, but many of these had been sadly neglected. The particular concern of the Reformers was to ensure that each parish should have a minister and Kirk Session with a responsibility for caring. These parishes were then grouped together on a geographical basis to constitute the "bounds" of the Presbyteries. The Presbyteries, in turn, were grouped to form the "provinces" of the Synods. And at the peak of the pyramid, of course, stood the General Assembly whose responsibility covered the entire country. Every court of the Church has, then, a territorial basis, it is firmly anchored to the land.

In early days Presbyteries were fairly small in extent and there were a lot of them. Towards the end of last century Mair records of the then Church of Scotland that "there are 84 Presbyteries; one includes 5 parishes, and one 94." As improved means of travel reduced distance the bounds of Presbyteries were extended so that they embraced more charges. At the time of the Union of the Churches in 1929 the courts of the two branches of the uniting Church were merged and reorganised to form 66 Presbyteries within Scotland. A major reshuffle was undertaken in 1975 at the time of the creation of the Regions and the general overhaul of local government in order that the boundaries of Presbyteries might substantially coincide with those of the new Districts, and this resulted in the total being reduced to 47. The recent union of two northern Presbyteries has brought the number today to 46, and there, I think, it may be expected to remain—for some time at least.

It would be unrealistic in a land where density of population varies so dramatically to imagine that Presbyteries could be of anything like comparable size. The number of charges varies from 9 to 182, but most Presbyteries fall within the 30-to-50 bracket. Even as things are there are areas where members of Presbytery are involved in over a hundred miles of motoring to attend a Presbytery meeting. A parish in the north can cover as many acres as does a whole Presbytery in the industrial belt.

In all of the above I have been talking exclusively of "home" Presbyteries—that is, those in Scotland. There was a time when the Church of Scotland had many charges across the border, as well as on the continent of Europe, and these, on the parallel of the situation at home, were grouped into Presbyteries. There was, too, a time when missionary outreach in Africa, India, etc. was on a more paternalistic basis than would be acceptable today, and all the charges in these continents were bound together to form Presbyteries. It will be readily recognised that these bodies were not Presbyteries in the strict sense of the term. For one thing they had no territorial basis.

Further, they did not enjoy that unique constitutional position under the law which over the centuries the Kirk has won for itself within its native shores. Of all of these "Presbyteries Furth of Scotland" (there were 19 of them fifty years ago) only three remain today. There is the Presbytery of England embracing in all nine widely-scattered charges; there is the Presbytery of Europe with altogether seven charges as far apart as Amsterdam and Malta; and there is the Presbytery of Jersusalem, and that is governed by a special Act of Assembly and has only three ministerial members.

In all that follows I am thinking of the Presbytery in Scotland. Most—but not all—of what I have to say will apply equally to the Presbytery of England, but the other two must be seen as special cases operating under their own particular legislation.

A Scottish Presbytery, then, has its "bounds", and its membership consists of ministers and elders from within these bounds. No-one can qualify as a member of Presbytery who is not either a minister or an elder, and as such he must have signed the Formula declaring his acceptance of and adherence to the Church's position in the matter of doctrine, government, and worship. Some years ago a proposal was made that deaconesses should be admitted to membership of Presbytery, but this was withdrawn in face of fairly strenuous opposition. Part of the platform of that opposition was that ordination was of the essence of membership of Presbytery and that deaconesses, not being ordained, were constitutionally barred. I do not, for my own part, lay much store by this argument, but certainly the *de facto* situation is that members of Presbytery are without exception ordained persons.

Members

Recent years have witnessed a complete reversal in the Church's attitude to the question of membership of Presbytery. In early times the guiding principle was the "exclusive" one—the right to sit in the court was a privilege reserved to as few as possible. In the case of retirement, for example, the senior minister continued in office as Minister of the Parish but had an Assistant and Successor appointed, and only the former (not the latter although it was he who was doing the work) could sit in Presbytery. Or again, the famous Stewarton case of 1843 decided that the ministers of the Chapels of Ease (the Church Extension charges of those days) were not entitled to membership. Today we have moved to an "inclusive" principle that wishes to gather into the Presbytery all who can be seen as having something to contribute to its deliberations. The legislation presently governing the situation is Act II 1970. In the last seven years there have been no fewer than five amending Acts passed, each extending still further the conditions entitling to membership.

Ministers

The classes of minister who are entitled to seats in Presbytery are the following—it being understood in every case, of course, that each holds the status of a minister of the Church of Scotland.

(a) A Minister of a charge within the bounds, whether inducted thereto or serving in a terminable appointment, and including a Collegiate Minister and an Associate Minister.

(b) A Minister holding an appointment as a Professor, Lecturer or Reader in a Faculty of Divinity of a University situated within the bounds.

(c) A Minister who has been appointed to a post overseas, so long as he has not come under the direction and control of the indigenous Church—the Presbytery being that of which he was a member at the time of his appointment, or of the Presbytery which ordained him for the post, or, if he were ordained overseas, of the Presbytery which licensed him.

(d) A Minister who holds a commission as Chaplain to H.M. Forces—the Presbytery being that within which he is serving whether at home or abroad, or, if he is serving where there is no Presbytery, of that which ordained him for the post or of which he was a member at the time of his commissioning.

(e) A Minister holding an appointment under a court or Committee of the Church—in which case he may choose the Presbytery (i) in which his office is situated, (ii) within whose bounds he works, or (iii) which includes the congregation to which he is attached.

(f) A Minister holding one of the appointments in the Schedule to Act II 1970—with the choice of Presbytery of place of work, of residence, or of worship.

(g) A Minister who has successfully petitioned the General Assembly for a seat in Presbytery. Unless the Assembly has ordained otherwise, he will have the choice of the Presbytery of his place of work or of worship.

(h) A Probationer who has been ordained Assistant attached to a charge within the bounds.

(i) A Minister from any of the above groups who has retired on grounds of age or infirmity or to facilitate readjustment, unless in the latter case he has taken up full-time service outwith the jurisdiction of the Church.

Two points have to be noted in regard to the final group above. First, that a recent Act (VIII, 1980) provides that a retired minister may, at will, resign his seat in Presbytery without in any way affecting his ministerial status. Secondly, that at no point in the legislation is any definition available as to what precisely constitutes "age or infirmity". At one time it meant simply "seventy or a doctor's certificate", but today, more and more, ministers are seeking retirement before reaching a stage which could fairly attract either of these traditional descriptions, and the provisions of the Retirement Scheme now make it possible to do so on modified pension terms. It is submitted that today a minister is to be regarded as entitled to retain his seat in Presbytery provided he has retired completely from full-time gainful employment, irrespective of his age or the condition of his health.

It might further be added of the retired minister that in terms of Act VII 1980 he may apply for transference to another Presbytery (if he moves house, for instance). This is effected simply by making written application to the Presbytery to which he wishes to move, and, in due course, by submitting to that Presbytery a Certificate from the Presbytery he is leaving.

Elders

It is an oft-quoted principle that "once an elder always an elder". I do not wish at this point to become embroiled in an argument as to exactly what this means, so let it suffice to say that for purposes of holding a seat in Presbytery only that elder is eligible who can produce from his Kirk Session a Certificate of *bona fide* Eldership—that is to say, he has to be an honest-to-goodness member of a Kirk Session within the bounds.

The representation of elders within the Presbytery is as set out hereunder.

(a) Each Kirk Session (whether linked or not) appoints one of its own number (or from any other Kirk Session within the bounds) to represent it in the Presbytery. In the case of a Collegiate charge two elders are to be appointed, but not so where there is an Associate Minister or an Ordained Assistant.

(b) The Presbytery itself elects additional Elders from within the membership of its Kirk Sessions, one elder in respect of each ministerial member who is not a Parish Minister or a Collegiate Minister.

(c) In terms of Act V 1980 the Presbytery may appoint further Additional Elders up to a maximum of one-third of its congregations.

It may be interjected here parenthetically that there is no officially accepted title for those elders who have been elected by Presbytery. Those appointed by Kirk Sessions are "Representative Elders", and for myself I have always called the others "Additional Elders", but I have no authority for this nomenclature and it is certainly not in universal use. I have seen the terms "Balancing Elder" and "Equalising Elder" but neither of these appeals to me.

Elders' Commissions run from 1st July to 30th June in each year, and Kirk Sessions are enjoined to meet within two months of the close of the General Assembly for the purpose of electing their Representative Elders. There is no reason why the election should not precede the close of the General Assembly, and it is a great convenience at the administrative level if it can be held as early as possible.

Should an elder appointed to the Presbytery die, or resign his eldership, or leave the membership of his congregation, or be disqualified, then the Kirk Session which appointed him or the Presbytery which elected him as the case may be, is entitled to appoint or elect another elder in his place. If the Kirk Session does not exercise this right within a month the Presbytery may itself elect an elder to fill the vacancy.

At the Union of the Churches in 1929 the principle was established of a strict numerical parity between ministers and elders in the membership of the Presbytery, and indeed of all the courts apart from the Session. The number of Additional Elders appointed by the Presbytery was strictly determined so as to achieve the position that, when the Roll of Presbytery was made up (say at 1st July), the two totals were identical. This meant that a linked charge had to be represented by one elder only, and he might be from either of the Kirk Sessions. He was chosen at a joint meeting of Sessions. This state of affairs was never really satisfactory. For one thing it meant that many Kirk Sessions knew little or nothing of what was happening at Presbytery level.

In any case, the "parity principle" was more apparent than real since, whatever might be the theory of the matter, the elders always enjoyed a numerical ascendancy, and, if they had wished to do so, they could easily have outvoted the ministers. There were two reasons for this—first, there were always vacant charges each represented by an elder but not by a minister, and, secondly, some at least of the retired ministers were members of Presbytery in name only but were offset by active elders.

It appeared, therefore, that no vital constitutional principle would be disturbed by allowing representation to each of the Kirk Sessions in a linking, and this

was done in 1977. And then in 1980, on the instigation of the Committee of Forty, power was given to
Presbyteries to elect still more Additional Elders up
to a maximum of one-third of the congregations within
the bounds. The Act says "shall elect" (not "may
elect"), but since no minimum figure is stipulated the
extent to which the power is exercised may be regarded
as wholly optional—and that is the same as to say that
it is up to the Presbytery to decide whether it wishes to
take advantage of it at all.

A question arises in my own mind as to whether the
comparative strength of the two elements is not,
perhaps, in need of review. I take a biggish Presbytery
(admittedly not typical) as a first example. Here there
are 42 charges, including 16 linkings, and with five of
the charges vacant. This means that there are 58
congregations. There are 36 ministers in non-parochial
appointments or retired, and of these 11 are completely
out of action. This gives a maximum ministerial voting
strength of 62. The number of elders, if the options
were all taken up, could be: 58 for parishes, 36
"additional" against extra ministers, and 20 more
(being a third of the number of congregations)—total
voting strength, 114. This works out at very nearly
two-to-one. Or I take a small Presbytery of 15 charges,
one vacant and 14 with linkings, and eight retired
ministers, four of them non-attending—giving a
ministerial maximum of 18. Elders could number: 29
(the number of parishes), 8 against retired ministers,
and 10 optional extras, giving a possible of 47. This is
considerably more than two-to-one. We have travelled
a long way from parity. Are we travelling too far?

A further point about which unhappiness is sometimes expressed has to do with how comparatively

small a proportion of the Presbytery consists of parish ministers. For example, in the earlier case just quoted vital decisions are being reached on issues which can lay heavy burdens upon the parish minister, and this is being done by a body of 176 members of whom these parish ministers represent a mere 37. Is this wise? And is it wholly fair?

Correspondents

In 1980 provision was officially made for inclusion within Presbyteries of certain Corresponding Members—a classification that had obtained within the General Assembly for a number of years. Corresponding Members are people "who shall have the right to attend all meetings of Presbytery and to speak on any matter that is before the court but shall not have the right to vote."

No rules are laid down regarding who may be granted this status or how many there may be—the only statutory provision being that Deaconesses and Lay Missionaries working within the bounds are to be Corresponding Members *ex officiis*. It is customary also to include some representation from the local Presbyterial Council of the Woman's Guild. Besides which the Diocesan Council of the Episcopal Church may be invited to appoint someone to attend in this capacity. The Presbytery may invite any member of another Presbytery present at its meeting to be a Corresponding Member.

Since Corresponding Members have no right to vote it follows that they have no power to propose or second motions. And since their speaking is to be confined to "any matter before the Presbytery" it seems to follow that they have no right to raise any new matter—

though it would seem not to be beyond human ingenuity if one of them wished to speak on some matter that was not likely to arise in the normal course for an abnormal course to be arranged!

Associates

It is customary at a meeting *in hunc effectum*—for an ordination or induction, or for the dedication of Church buildings, for example—to agree to associate with the Presbytery for that meeting members of other Presbyteries who may be present, as also ministers of other denominations whose orders are recognised by the Church of Scotland. Since these are not meetings at which ordinary business is being transacted the question of the powers of such Associates is of little significance. It is customary that they should be welcomed by the Moderator, and that their presence should be recorded in the minute.

Assessors

Though it rarely happens today, the General Assembly has power to appoint Assessors to act with a Presbytery either for specific business or for the conduct of its affairs in general. Whether or not such Assessors have a judicial vote will depend on the specific terms of their appointment. The last occasion I can recall of such an appointment was when the then Presbytery of Islay had been so reduced in numbers that it was difficult (and sometimes impossible) for it to carry through its necessary Presbyterial functions. To assist in this situation Assessors were appointed and continued to act until the Presbytery was united with others to form the Presbytery of Southern Argyll.

Officials

For the efficient ordering of its affairs a Presbytery appoints a number of "officials"—normally the following.

Moderator The appointment of Moderator is governed by Act XXI of 1944 which provides that he is to be chosen by free election from among the ministerial members of the court, that he is to hold office for at least a year, and that he may be re-elected for a second term. Up to that time it had been customary for the appointment to be made on a strict rota basis and to last usually for only six months.

In the absence of the Moderator a previous Moderator, whom failing the senior minister present, takes the chair. In case of the death of the Moderator or of his translation to a charge in another Presbytery, the duties devolve upon his predecessor until the Presbytery can meet and make a fresh appointment. It is not unusual for the Presbytery when appointing a meeting *in hunc effectum* to nominate a Moderator *pro tempore* to preside thereat.

The Moderator is responsible for calling—or for refusing to call—a special meeting of the court when requisitioned to do so by three members (see "Meetings *pro re nata*" on page 21).

It is the duty of the Moderator to cause good order to be kept, to rule on points of order, to refuse to accept motions which are incompetent, irrelevant, or offensive. It is for him to declare the result of a vote. If a point of order is raised the Moderator may hear members speak on the question, but there shall be no vote taken—the decision is the Moderator's alone. Once he has ruled, however, his ruling becomes a judgment of the court and is subject to appeal like any other.

The Moderator signs, along with the Clerk, all minutes of the Presbytery which are approved at the meeting over which he presides. He also signs, with the Clerk, any petition, overture, or other document being transmitted in name of the Presbytery to a superior court. His signature is not required on extract minutes of the Presbytery.

Clerk   The Presbytery appoints someone to act as its Clerk. The person so appointed is generally a minister, but this is not invariably the case. It is in order to appoint as Clerk someone who is not a member of the court, though I have never known this to happen, and I imagine it would prove extremely inconvenient. Occasionally more than one Clerk is appointed. Before assuming office the Clerk takes the oath *de fidele administratione*. He holds office during the will of the Presbytery. In certain of the larger Presbyteries the appointment is on a full-time basis. Even when this is so the office is held at the will of the court.

In the absence of the regular clerk from any meeting an appointment is made of a Clerk *pro tempore* and he takes the oath *de fidele*. No matter how formal the business is to be, a meeting should never be held in the absence of an Acting Clerk duly appointed and sworn. This should be attended to immediately the meeting is constituted and the facts of the appointment and the oath should appear in the minute.

The Clerk is the custodier of the Presbytery's records and he alone is entitled to give extracts therefrom. An interesting survival of an ancient practice is that anyone appealing against a Presbytery decision "takes instruments in the Clerk's hands and craves extracts." The point is more fully elaborated under the subject of "Appeal" on page 131.

The Clerk takes minutes of all meetings of Presbytery, sees to it that copies of these are circulated before the next meeting, and, once they have been approved, appends his signature along with that of the Moderator. He is responsible for ensuring that copies of loose-leaf minutes are bound in permanent form as soon as a suitable number of loose-leaves has accumulated.

Treasurer Most Presbyteries appoint a Treasurer, though in some cases the Clerk fulfils these duties along with his own. A layman may be, and very often is, appointed to this post. The oath *de fidele* should be administered when he takes office.

Officer The Presbytery usually appoints an Officer to wait on its meetings and to execute its orders— normally a layman who is not a member of the court. One of his most useful functions is to take charge of seating arrangements, procession, etc. at a special meeting. On appointment he undertakes to carry out his duties with fidelity. He receives a salary determined by the Presbytery.

Precentor To "give the note" at the Presbytery's opening devotions a member of the court is chosen to act as Precentor. Musical ability counting for more than status in a holder of this office, an elder is often chosen.

3

How It Does Its Work

The point has already been made that a Presbytery
has "bounds". It also has a "seat"—that is, the place
where it meets for the transaction of regular business.
In days past this was generally the principal town
within the bounds, which also gave its name to the
Presbytery; but today it is becoming increasingly
common for a Presbytery to have its "seat" in some
village which is centrally situated to serve the area
as a whole—Innerleithen for Melrose and Peebles,
Glenluce for Wigtown and Stranraer, Monquhitter for
Buchan are examples that spring to mind. The
advantages from the point of view of parking must be
obvious enough, even if accessibility for the non-
motorist is not so clear.

Most of the post-1929 Presbyteries represented the
union of the corresponding courts from the two
branches of the Church, and while they covered
practically the same bounds they often had different
seats. In many cases by way of compromise both seats
were retained in use and a double-barrelled name
adopted, some meetings being held in one seat and
some in the other. The plan, like most compromises,
was never an especially happy one, and I think that
within the last few years all such systems have been
departed from.

There are no statutory obligations governing the occasion or frequency of Presbytery meetings, beyond the fact that the court must meet once a year to fix a meeting when it is going to select its commissioners to the General Assembly and must subsequently meet so to do. The general pattern, however, is that Presbyteries meet from seven to eleven times a year, usually on a fixed day such as the second Tuesday of the month. In the more populous areas these meetings are always held in the evening to make it easier for elders to attend. In the more remote parts where distance creates its own problems Presbyteries still meet during the day.

Types of Meeting

There are three kinds of way in which a Presbytery may meet, and there are no other.

Ordinary Meeting   First there is the "ordinary" or "regular" meeting sometimes erroneously referred to as "the statutory meeting". I say "erroneously" because the designation "statutory meeting" refers properly to a meeting held in obedience to a statute, that is, an enactment passed by a superior court. Now the fact that a Presbytery agrees in its Standing Orders to meet on certain specific days does not constitute such a statute. At an ordinary meeting all regular business can be transacted.

A most important feature about the ordinary meeting is that before its conclusion the Presbytery must appoint the time and place of its next ordinary meeting, and must give public intimation of this. The fact that everybody present knows that the next

meeting is "a month today in the hall here" is of no
consequence—a solemn resolution in regard to the
matter has got to be reached, recorded, and pro-
claimed. This having been done at some point in the
course of the proceedings the court, when it reaches
the end of its agenda, "adjourns to meet at . . . . on . . . .
at . . . . . o'clock." The result is that a Presbytery is
always either sitting or standing adjourned, and if it
allows itself to fall, as it were, between these two stools
then its powers and functions lapse and it has to be
"revived". This involves a fairly complicated process whereby not fewer than three members have
to requisition the Moderator to call a meeting of
Presbytery *pro re nata* from ten to fifteen days from
the date of the requisition for the sole purpose of
appointing a regular meeting at which the court may
be "revived" and its ordinary business put in hand.
Not only so, an explanation of the whole affair has to be
submitted to the first meeting of Synod, and there is a
liability that the Presbytery may incur the censure of
that court if the circumstances appear to merit it.

While it cannot accurately be called an "ordinary
meeting", the Presbytery may meet for the transaction
of ordinary business in consequence of an order of the
General Assembly or of the Synod. I state this on the
authority of Cox (6th Edition page 149), but I have not
myself ever known of this occurring and if it did I
should expect it to be for the transaction of some item of
business clearly specified and not for all ordinary
affairs.

Unless with special permission of the court
concerned, a Presbytery is not to meet while the
General Assembly or the local Synod is in session. This
should, I am sure, be interpreted as prohibiting a

meeting even after the superior court has risen but at an hour which does not conveniently allow of members attending in both places. Presbyteries within fifty miles of Edinburgh are prohibited from meeting during the sittings of the General Assembly or on the day appointed for their Commission. By the same token it could be said, in parentheses, Kirk Sessions are not to meet, nor are congregational meetings to be held, when an ordinary meeting of Presbytery is in session.

Meeting in hunc effectum When a particular item of business has to be undertaken by the Presbytery— ordination or induction of a minister, dedication of a Church building, the licensing of students—the court will normally arrange for this to be done at a meeting *in hunc effectum* ("for that purpose"). The time and place of the proposed meeting have to be fixed, intimated, and minuted at a regular meeting, as has also the business to be undertaken, and only that business can be legally transacted.

It is not unusual for the Presbytery to find that at an *in hunc effectum* meeting fixed for an induction it would be convenient to deal also with some other item—of vacancy business perhaps. This is perfectly in order so long as the addition to the agenda is agreed at an ordinary meeting. The only exception to this rule is that an elder's commission may be received and sustained at any meeting, including a meeting *in hunc effectum*.

Meeting pro re nata In the event that some item of urgent and important business arises between ordinary meetings and demands to be dealt with without delay it lies within the discretion of the Moderator to call a meeting *pro re nata* ("for a thing that has come into being"). If requisitioned to do so by not fewer than

three members of the court the Moderator is bound to
call such a meeting, or answer for his failure so to do. In
the event of the death of the Moderator these duties
devolve upon the Clerk. The meeting is called by a
circular letter addressed by the Moderator to all the
members, distinctly setting forth the business for
which it is called. The first item on the agenda at such a
meeting is to approve the conduct of the Moderator in
having called it. If approval is not forthcoming then the
meeting is closed there and then: if approval is given
the specific item of business is dealt with and the
meeting is closed. In either case the facts are reported
at the first ordinary meeting and it is in order for
anyone so minded though he had not been at the
meeting to take exception to its having been called, and
indeed to pursue his complaint to a higher court. At
that stage, however, nothing that he can do can upset
the finality of the judgments reached at the meeting.

It is well accepted that a meeting *pro re nata* can be
called only by the Moderator and involves the
despatch of a circular letter. Nothing is said in so many
words as to who is to sign the letter. My own view is
that it should be a letter over the signature of the
Moderator—at least that is the safest way. A letter over
the signature of the Clerk, saying, "I am instructed by
the Moderator to call . . . ." may well be adequate,
but I think it could still be open to challenge. A letter
from the Clerk saying simply, "A meeting *pro re nata* is
to be held . . . . " would in my view be quite inept.

Meeting on Death of a Minister   On the occasion of the
death of the minister of a parish the Presbytery meets
within the Church concerned on the day of the funeral
without necessarily having received notice, and it
appoints an interim moderator to act with the Session

in arranging pulpit supply, and transacts any other urgent business consequent upon the death. This is strictly a meeting *pro re nata* (however inappropriate the "nata" may be), but it does not require to be summoned by letter nor to be formally approved. It is usual practice today for a newspaper advertisement to appear giving notice of such a meeting.

This may be an appropriate point at which to state that it is only in the case of the death of a parish minister that the Presbytery convenes on the occasion of the funeral. Such a minister has no pastor of his own to officiate at the funeral and the Presbytery acts for him in this capacity. In the case of retired ministers and of ministers holding appointments other than parochial charges the arrangements for the funeral lie with the next of kin. Members of Presbytery will, naturally, wish to attend such a funeral and may, where appropriate, wish to sit as a body, but the Presbytery will not be constituted. The occurrence of the death will be recorded at the first ordinary meeting thereafter.

Meeting in Committee To allow for a wider freedom of discussion than is always possible under the pressures of an ordinary meeting, a Presbytery may resolve to meet "in committee" or "in conference" under the chairmanship of the Moderator or of some other person appointed for the purpose. This normally would be done in a case where some important issue of public policy had arisen or where a matter had been sent down by the Assembly for consideration and comment.

At such a meeting resolutions may be framed and voted upon, but such resolutions have, of course, no authority or value until they have been ratified—as

normally they will be—when the report of the meeting
in committee is given in at the first ordinary meeting
thereafter. Cox states that at a meeting in committee
"the ordinary rules of debate are understood to be
suspended". While this may be true it is well to
remember that the rules of debate were devised to
facilitate, not to impede, discussion, and that the
dangers inherent in too much freedom are likely to be
greater than those arising from a strict observance of
the rules. A free-for-all is likely to prove entertaining
rather than edifying.

Need for Care   Before leaving the subject of the ways
in which a Presbytery may meet it should prove
interesting (even instructive) to recount an incident
which actually occurred some years ago. The meeting
had dragged on rather wearily and when at length the
last item had been disposed of the Moderator nipped in
smartly and pronounced the benediction. While the
brethren were yet raising their heads the Clerk
interjected—"The next meeting will be held here a
month today at the usual hour." When in due course
the papers for this meeting were circulated the Clerk
received a letter from one of the ministers—every
Presbytery has one of the kind, fortunate indeed if it
has only one—saying that he was interested to note
there was to be an informal gathering of ministers and
elders held next week but that he did not intend to be
present. He went on to explain that since it had
concluded its business and been closed with prayer
without having appointed the time and place for its
next meeting the Presbytery had now lapsed.

The Moderator and Clerk regretfully agreed that the
matter had better be taken seriously. The fathers and
brethren having come together from far and wide were

surprised, not to say disappointed, to learn that they were no longer a Presbytery! After some discussion on the procedure involved three of them requisitioned the Moderator to call a meeting *pro re nata* when a proper meeting could be appointed and they could get on with the business of the court. Meantime they all went home—unusually early.

Unhappily the letter calling the *pro re nata* meeting went out over the name of the Clerk. This elicited from the difficult brother a letter to the effect that he noted they were now forming a club and holding regular meetings, but that he had no intention of joining! Once again the fathers and brethren converged from far and near only to learn of the new problem. This time they took the view that "enough is enough" and that they should get on with the business—which they did—I incline to think quite irregularly. When it was represented to the difficult one that if dissatisfied he should take his case to the Assembly, he replied that the latter was a corrupt court since it would include persons masquerading as commissioners from the non-existent Presbytery of Auchterloonie! Maybe the Presbytery had something when it decided that enough is enough.

It's safer—even if much less interesting—to play the game according to the rules, however stupid these may appear.

General Rules

Quorum   The quorum of the Presbytery, irrespective of its size, is three, of whom at least two must be ministers. This total includes the Moderator.

In Public   While the Kirk Session always meets in private all the other courts of the Church meet in public unless for special reason it is resolved "to sit alone", or "behind closed doors", or just "in private". Reports on quinquennial visitation are required by the relevant Act to be heard in private, and there are occasions when it is clearly desirable to deal with some disciplinary matters in the absence of spectators. In my own view the Presbytery should resort to the private session only very occasionally and for compelling reason. A Presbytery of the Kirk in Scotland is a court of the land and its business is presumed to be of public concern. In the words of Lord President Inglis the Presbytery is "an established judicature of the country as much recognised by law as the Court of Session itself". Or again, Lord Justice Clerk Moncreiff, "The jurisdiction of the Church courts ... rests upon a similar statutory foundation to that under which we administer justice within these walls." A court of this nature has no right to shut its doors unless for very adequate reason. By needlessly huddling in corners, it seems to me, we put at risk our unique status. The fact that the Presbytery is a court of the land is the reason, incidentally, why public intimation has always to be made of the time and place of its meetings, and why provision has to be made (physically) for the attendance of the public should they desire to be present.

Let us be frank and admit that no-one seriously expects the public to attend, at least in any numbers. But today, it must be recognised, the attendance of "the press" symbolises the presence and concern of the public. It is often suggested that the debate on some delicate theme will be conducted more freely in the absence of the boys-with-the-pencils and that the court should accordingly resolve to meet in private. Two things are to be borne in mind here. First that if you turn the press out they will know for sure there is something afoot they would want to be reporting and they will not likely encounter too much difficulty in discovering what that is. Secondly that the presence of the reporters can impose upon the discussion an element of restraint and responsibility that will generally be very much to its advantage.

Standing Orders   Most Presbyteries have their own Standing Orders affecting such things as their committee structure and their time and place of meeting and also covering some of the rules of debate. The general rule in this field is that when any situation is not covered by the Standing Orders of the court concerned those of the next superior court apply. This in effect generally means that debate in Presbytery is governed by the Standing Orders of the General Assembly. Most Presbyteries have a Standing Order (which would not be appropriate in the Assembly) that no matter on which a final judgment has been reached can be brought up again within six months (see also page 145).

Notice of Motion   There are certain matters which can be determined by a Presbytery only if notice has been given at a previous meeting—the appointment of commissioners to the General Assembly, voting on Overtures sent down under the Barrier Act, any alterations to Standing Orders, are examples. Apart from these it is a sound rule that an important issue should never be sprung on the court—least of all at the close of a meeting under the heading of "Any Other Competent Business", when those members who have not already gone home are wearying to do so.

If, then, anyone has a motion which he wishes to propose on any matter of moment he should give notice of the terms of his proposed motion and ask that at the next meeting a place be found on the agenda when he may move accordingly. It is not unusual to accept the circulation along with the papers of the print of a proposed motion as an adequate substitute for notice properly given in, but if the matter is one of considerable importance and there is no call for haste then I think this is a practice not to be encouraged. In my opinion a person who has given in timely notice should be at liberty to amend the terms of his motion when he comes to propose it, so long as the change is not so revolutionary as to make it in effect a completely new motion.

In Writing Any motion proposed at a Presbytery meeting should be handed to the Clerk in writing, and anyone having it in mind to move on any matter that is to be before the meeting would be well advised to come prepared in this regard. It must be recognised, at the same time, that anyone trying to work out a compromise solution of some tricky issue that has developed in the course of the debate can scarcely be expected to produce writing on demand, so that time has to be allowed to get it committed to writing, and it is a good thing if the debate be halted while this is being done. Certainly before a vote is taken on any matter the Clerk should be in a position to read out the precise terms of all the motions, counter-motions, and amendments that are to be voted on. Incidentally— and I speak from experience—there are few things more exasperating for a Clerk than to hear a speaker bring a long rambling peroration to a close with the words, "And I beg to move accordingly."

Order of the Day Occasionally a Presbytery fixes an Order of the Day for some particular item—a question of especial importance, or a case involving the presence of parties, for example. What this means is that when the appointed time comes the court will continue the item of business on hand to its conclusion and then pass immediately to the matter of the "order". In the event that the business on hand has not been concluded half-an-hour after the time fixed, it will be suspended, and resumed only after the item covered by the "order" has been completely disposed of.

Conduct of Business

Devotions An ordinary meeting of Presbytery is invariably opened with devotions, including praise (custom dictates that this be from the metrical psalms or paraphrases and be led by a precentor), the reading of Scripture, and prayer, and is conducted by the Moderator who, however, is at liberty to invite someone to assist him. At other than ordinary meetings it is usual simply to constitute with prayer. It is well established that the pronouncing of the benediction by the Moderator is equivalent to "closing with prayer".

Sederunt The first item of business is to take the sederunt of the meeting. It is usual to do this by arranging that members on entering shall sign a Sederunt Book or shall strike off their names on a printed list. In smaller Presbyteries it is customary to print the sederunt in full in the minute, and I think that even in the larger Presbyteries this is done in the case of non-regular meetings. Where this would prove cumbersome it is usual to print a few names—enough to show beyond doubt that there had been a quorum —and then to refer to a Sederunt Book. It should be particularly noted that in such a case the Sederunt Book forms an integral part of the record and should be carefully preserved.

Roll of Presbytery A report is next given by the Clerk regarding any changes that have occurred in the Roll of Presbytery since last ordinary meeting, any elders' commissions submitted in that period are sustained, and a welcome is extended by the Moderator to new members if any.

Minutes Minutes of the last ordinary meeting and of any special meetings held subsequently are then submitted. Time was when these had to be read laboriously through, but today they are invariably (I think) printed or stencilled and have been circulated along with the papers for the meeting. So the minutes are "taken as read" and are approved, subject, if need be, to amendment.

When amendments are made (unless they be of the most trivial nature) the fact should be recorded in full in the minute of the meeting at which they are amended. It is not, in my opinion, enough to record, "The minutes of 10th October were submitted and, after adjustment, were approved." Under such a system an unscrupulous Clerk would be free to do to the minute such adjusting as he thought fit, and at a later date there would be nothing on record against which to check what had been done. Not that there are unscrupulous clerks, but blank signed cheques are dangerous temptations. It doesn't need a large-scale adjustment—the omission of the word "not" could be sufficient! The record should read, "The minutes of 10th October were submitted and, subject in the last line of page 123 to the substitution of the words '.......' in place of the words '......', were approved." In this way, and in this way alone, every member of the court who retains his copies of the minutes as circulated has a complete and trustworthy record of all Presbytery business—and to this, I maintain, he is entitled.

Once a minute has been approved and signed no part of it can be deleted or expunged for any reason whatever except on the order of a superior court. Nor can the accuracy of such a minute be challenged—the minute represents what happened at the meeting, whatever you may recollect to the contrary—and however clearly you may recollect it.

A motion which has failed to find a seconder is not recorded in the minute.

When any particularly complicated or contentious matter is before the Presbytery it is prudent that a draft minute should be framed as soon as the item is concluded and that this be read over, adjusted if need be, and approved. It will, in due course, be engrossed in the minute proper.

There used to be a rule that rubrics—that is, headings written in the margin—were essential in a minute. It is still as important today as ever it was that minutes should lend themselves to easy reference, but this can be better achieved by the skilful use of cross headings throughout the body of the text. In my opinion the heading, like its predecessor the rubric, should not have to be read as part of the text—that is to say, the minute should be complete and self-explanatory even if the heading is omitted.

Minutes should invariably be signed by the Moderator and the Clerk acting at the meeting at which they are approved whether or not they had been present at the meeting whose business is recorded. By their signatures they are testifying to the fact that to their knowledge the minutes have been approved— and to nothing more.

Parties in appeals etc. are entitled to extract minutes of those parts of the record concerned with their affairs. It is customary also to send a copy of the relevant extract to all who have had business before the Presbytery or whose interests are affected by its decisions. Others desiring extracts may have these only on the express authority of the court. The issuing of extracts is the business of the Clerk who alone has power to certify them as true. To be valid such an extract must begin by stating when and where the Presbytery was met and that it was duly constituted.

Tributes   It is usual for the Moderator at some point fairly early in the proceedings to pay tribute to the memory of any member who may have died since the last time of meeting.

Order of Business   Before the court engages upon its business proper it is a most useful thing for it to agree upon the items of business with which it is going to deal and the order in which they are to be taken. This will normally be proposed by the Convener of the Business Committee and will reflect the order in which the items appear on the agenda which has been circulated. At this point it is for anyone so minded to propose that some item should be brought forward, or that some other change should be made in the order. What is more important, perhaps, is that anyone who wishes to raise at that meeting some matter not on the agenda

must at this stage ask for a place on the order-paper
where he may do so—or remain forever silent. In this
way that most dangerous item on so many agenda,
"Any Other Competent Business" can be deleted—for
all the competent business will already have been
awarded a place, and any business other than that will
ipso facto not be "competent business".

Appointment of Next Meeting   While it is usual to fix
the time and place of next meeting immediately before
adjourning there is no reason why it should not be
included among the more or less formal business at the
beginning of the meeting. In this way the danger of its
being overlooked and the Presbytery lapsing is
minimised (see pages 20 and 24). In passing let me say
that the notice which accompanies the agenda and the
minutes is often spoken of as "the notice calling the
meeting". This is erroneous and misleading. The
meeting was "called" at some point during the
previous sederunt when the time and place were fixed
for it, and the notice is no more than a reminder which
should properly read, "Members are reminded of the
meeting of Presbytery appointed to be held . . . . . ."

Committee Reports   To facilitate the discharge of its
responsibilities a Presbytery normally appoints a
number of Committees, corresponding more or less to
those of the General Assembly. In particular there will
be a Business Committee to supervise the business of
the Presbytery itself, a Committee on the Maintenance
of the Ministry to look after Vacancy Schedules
and stipend matters generally, a Committee to
oversee Students for the Ministry, a Readjustments
Committee, a Youth Committee, and so on. As well as
these Standing Committees a Presbytery may well
appoint an *ad hoc* committee to advise upon some

matter sent down from the Assembly or some issue of local concern. A very great deal of the time and concern of today's Presbytery is occupied in receiving and debating the reports of its Committees.

Vacancy Business The other item of business likely to appear regularly on the agenda has to do with vacancies—the election, translation, and demission of ministers. All of this will be dealt with more fully hereunder (pages 38ff)—it is mentioned here merely to complete the list of likely business.

Assessments

Presbytery Dues The "running" of a Presbytery involves expenditure—printing, postage, telephone, salaries, rental of premises, and the like. It is usual for the Treasurer to prepare a budget for the coming year and to have this approved by the Presbytery. A system exists in each Presbytery by which the total is allocated out among the various congregations. The principles embodied in the system vary enormously—some are simple, some elaborate—but the object in each case is that of providing a formula which will share the load fairly among congregations, having regard to their size, financial potential, etc. Congregational Treasurers are informed and the Presbytery Dues become a first charge on all ordinary congregational income.

Assembly Dues The "running" of the General Assembly is no less an expensive item today. The General Finance Committee has a formula whereby the total requirements for "General Purposes" are shared out among all the Presbyteries, and these assessments are approved by the General Assembly itself. After that it is for the Presbytery, presumably on the same formula as with its own assessment, to do its divisions and to act as collector and transmitter.

It should be noted that a great deal of thought is presently being given to the possibility of introducing an "annual co-ordinated budget for the work of the Church" (which would take account of Ministry, of Mission and Service, and of General Purposes), and also of a "co-ordinated system for allocating the total budget among the congregations of the Church". This would cope with Assembly, but not, I imagine, with Presbytery, Dues.

4

What It Works At

SUPERVISING CONGREGATIONS

In the famous Act of Parliament of 1592 which established the Presbyterian system it is laid down that it belongs to the Presbytery to see that the "Word of God is purely preached within its bounds, the Sacraments rightly administered, and the discipline entertenyit." This is still today a fair enough summary of the business of the Presbytery, even if it does involve a vastly different programme from what it did a century ago, and still more from what it did in 1592.

It will prove convenient, I think, to gather the business of the Presbytery under the four general headings of (1) oversight of congregational activities, (2) oversight of ministers and other agents of the Church and of students of divinity, (3) its responsibilities as a court of appeal, reviewing decisions of others, and (4) its obligations towards the superior courts.

I begin, then, with the oversight of congregations, trying to trace, in as orderly a fashion as I can, the points at which the Presbytery has a duty to take a hand in the activities of congregations within its bounds.

Vacancy

The Presbytery has a special responsibility towards a congregation that is without a minister.

Occurrence of a Vacancy A congregation becomes vacant on the day of the death, deposition, demission, or translation of its minister, and, by order of the Presbytery, there is read from the pulpit on the first convenient Sunday after the occurrence of any of these an intimation declaring the charge to be vacant. In the case where the minister is demitting on account of age or for ill-health or to enable him to accept an appointment other than a charge, or where the minister is being translated to another parish, some time always elapses between the Presbytery agreeing to the demission or translation and the actual occurrence of the event in question. It can even extend to a period of some months. With a view to reducing the length of the vacancy the Presbytery will normally agree to treat such a case as one of "anticipated vacancy", thereby allowing the business of seeking a new minister to proceed—as far, indeed, as choosing a nominee—although the vacancy has still not in fact occurred.

Interim Moderator Immediately after the death or deposition of a minister or when it is agreed that a minister should demit or be translated, the Presbytery appoints one of its ministerial members to act as interim moderator in the vacancy in the one case, in the anticipated vacancy in the other. Usually the choice will be of a neighbouring minister, though care has to be taken not to pick one likely to be involved in subsequent readjustment negotiations. The Presbytery may appoint a retired minister, but not if he is a member of the vacant congregation, and it is unwise that a retired minister appointed interim moderator should also act as *locum tenens* in the vacancy. It is the duty of the interim moderator, so far as possible and consistently with his own work, to fill the place of the absent minister, and in particular to preside at all meetings of Kirk Session and congregation, and, in conference with the Kirk Session, to arrange for the supply of the vacant pulpit and for the provision of necessary pastoral services. He will also arrange with the Kirk Session to have the Electoral Register prepared and submitted to the Presbytery for attestation. If specifically asked to do so he may act as Convener of the Vacancy Committee but has no vote, casting or deliberative, in that capacity.

Question of Readjustment Simultaneously with the appointment of the interim moderator the question of readjustment is held to be raised. This aspect of vacancy procedure is dealt with hereunder (page 63). For the present let it be assumed that permission has been given to proceed to call a minister with or without restriction of choice.

Sustaining the Election Once the Vacancy Committee has made its selection of a nominee and the congregation has had the opportunity of voting, then, assuming the nominee has been duly elected and a Call subscribed, the matter has now to come to the Presbytery whose business it is to "sustain the appointment and call". The various papers, including the Call, have to be transmitted by the interim moderator to the Presbytery Clerk who then arranges for the matter to go on the agenda for the first convenient ordinary meeting. The Clerk also arranges that an edict be served citing the congregation to appear at the said meeting "for their interest". When the time comes the various documents are laid on the table, a representative of the congregation is heard on the theme of how Mr P.Q. is the minister of their dreams, there is a call for objections, parties are removed, and a motion to sustain is carried without discussion.

It was not always so. Time was when Presbyteries took a most lively interest in the choice which congregations made. There are on record many instances where the Presbytery refused to sustain a call because they considered "that the said Mr P.Q. was unmeet to edify" in that particular parish, or because they thought his record did not commend him for that appointment. So far as I am aware it would still be competent for a Presbytery to take this line, but the invariable practice is for the court to satisfy itself on the four questions—(1) Has the correct procedure been scrupulously adhered to? (2) Is the person elected properly qualified for the appointment? (3) Has there been no undue pressure or unfair influence exerted in any quarter to achieve the Call? (4) Is the number of signatures on the Call such as to promise reasonably loyal support for the new minister? If the answers to all of these questions are in the affirmative the election and call will surely be sustained without ado. It may be that someone is wondering whether the person is the ideal one to make a success of that particular parish and to work amicably with these particular people, but today he will keep these questions very much to himself.

Sometimes there can be hesitation on the part of the Presbytery if it seems that the Call is inadequately signed. Few Calls today bear more than the signatures of half of those on the Electoral Register. The Presbytery may send the Call back for further signatures, and this has been known to have had a salutary effect on a congregation in a lackadaisical state of indifference. There is, of course, a difficulty about sending back the Call. The law says that the document is to "lie for signatures" on a number of occasions and it forbids its being canvassed around the congregation. If, then, the elders, in response to its being returned, take the Call around their districts they are legally at fault, while if they merely arrange for it to "lie" for a while longer the chances of securing more signatures are probably remote. An awkward dilemma. In any case, if the congregation is in that state of "couldn't care less" then the sooner they get a minister—and a good one at that—the better!

The Presbytery, having sustained the election, will go on to make arrangements for the induction of the person concerned—provisional arrangements if he is already minister of a charge.

Translation   Should the person elected be minister of a parish the Presbytery, on sustaining the election, will go on to make arrangements to have the call "prosecuted" before the Presbytery to which he belongs. Until comparatively recent times this involved appointing commissioners to attend a meeting of that Presbytery where they would be heard on the subject of why the translation should be agreed to. At one time this was of crucial importance, for the Presbytery might well decide that the minister in question was doing an excellent job where he was and his ministry there should not be disturbed. His own congregation had, of course, been cited to the meeting and they might well resist his going. Today either ministers are less popular in their congregations or there is wider recognition of the fact that when a man is set on moving there's little point in trying to keep him, for the almost universal practice is that the Clerk of the "calling" Presbytery transmits the relevant documents to his counterpart in the "translating" Presbytery, the about-to-be-deprived congregation appear and "concur with reluctance" in his departure, and his translation is thereupon unanimously approved. An extract minute is sent to the Clerk of the "calling" Presbytery and the provisional arrangements that had been made for induction become operative.

"The Five-Year Rule" Disturbed by the fact that in many cases ministers were staying for only a very short time in their first charges, the Assembly of 1959 passed an Act (XXIV) making it illegal for a Presbytery to agree to the translation of a minister who was in his first parish and had not completed five years therein. At the same time the Act allowed for the existence of "exceptional circumstances" which would justify an exception being made in a particular case. To avoid the unhappy situation bound to arise were the matter to go as far as the releasing Presbytery before being challenged, the Act laid the responsibility upon the interim moderator in the vacancy to ensure that, before such a person were nominated, he (the interim moderator) would have in his hand a certificate from the releasing Presbytery (or from certain of its officials) to the effect that there were exceptional circumstances in this case.

Naturally enough the Act did not attempt to define "exceptional circumstances" and unfortunately one or two rather glaring instances occurred where the only extraordinary feature seemed to be the prestigious nature of the calling congregation. In consequence it has been found difficult to enforce the conditions in other cases. It is still, however, the duty of the releasing Presbytery to act responsibly in this situation and to interpret "extraordinary" in a reasonable way.

Induction   No man can become minister of a parish until he has been inducted to it by the Presbytery, and, once inducted, he continues in that office until his pastorate has been terminated either by death or by an act of the Presbytery in deposing, translating, or accepting demission. Neither minister nor congregation can, unilaterally or even by joint agreement, sever the tie that induction has created between them. Even if a minister disappears from his parish he continues to be minister of it until the Presbytery has declared him to be in desertion and has deposed him in consequence.

Ad vitam aut culpam   The General Assembly of 1972 accepted, with what in my view was amazingly little hostility, a quite revolutionary Act which provides that, "As from the date of the passing of this Act a minister of the Church of Scotland admitted or inducted to a charge shall not be admitted or inducted *ad vitam aut culpam* but except as hereinafter provided on attaining the age of 70 years, his ministry shall terminate as if he had resigned his charge and such date been appointed by the Presbytery of the bounds for the demission by the minister of his charge." The Act goes on to allow for the minister to be employed on a *de diem in diem* basis, presumably in his former charge if the Presbytery so determines, and to preserve the *ad vitam aut culpam* rights of all ministers inducted before the passing of the Act. A subsequent Act a couple of years later made it clear "for the avoidance of doubt" that when a man became minister of what could be regarded as a new charge in consequence of the charge to which he had been inducted being involved in readjustment his right to continue *ad vitam aut culpam* was not to be disturbed.

For my own part I think it is unfortunate that the Act is framed as it is, for it seems to bring *ad vitam aut culpam* as the basis of ministry to an end without putting anything in its place when all that in fact it is doing is to provide that instead of induction establishing a pastorate that can be ended only by death or deposition there is to be a new qualification—the attainment of the age of seventy.

Service of Induction As indicated above, when a Presbytery has sustained a call it proceeds to make arrangements for an induction. If the Call is addressed to a Probationer it will be an ordination and induction. A meeting *in hunc effectum* is appointed to be held in the vacant Church—one of the Churches in the case of linked congregations—and members of Presbytery are selected to take part. Immediately at the close of the service, the Presbytery having returned to the hall, three things occur—first, certified intimation of the induction is delivered by the Presbytery Clerk to the Session Clerk to be engrossed in the minute of the first meeting of Session thereafter; secondly, the Presbytery Clerk delivers to the new minister an extract minute of the Maintenance of the Ministry Committee setting forth the financial terms of his appointment; and thirdly, the Presbytery agrees to the addition of the name of the new minister to the Roll of the Presbytery.

Edict Before the service of induction begins, however, there is an important item of business to be transacted. When the date of induction was fixed the Presbytery Clerk arranged for an edict to be served in the vacant Church (or Churches) on the two

immediately preceding Sundays recounting the fact of
the election, stating the Presbytery's intention to
proceed to the induction "unless something occur
which may reasonably impede it", and calling on all
concerned that if they or any of them have anything to
object to in the life or doctrine of the said Mr So-and-So
they are to appear before a meeting of the Presbytery
which is to be held at a specific time stated—generally
a little while earlier than the hour fixed for the
induction service.

Further intimation of this meeting is made by the
Presbytery Officer, or other person appointed for
the purpose, once the Presbytery is in session.
Traditionally this intimation was made at "the most
patent door" of the Church. Today it is generally made
inside the Church to the assembling congregation. In
many ways this is unfortunate, for the older method
underlined, even if only symbolically, the important
fact that the minister is being inducted to the parish
and not just to the congregation, and that, in
consequence, what is about to take place concerns
those outside no less than it does those assembled
within.

I have never in my own experience known of an
objector appearing, but I have often wondered how
one ought to react should such a thing occur—as it
perfectly well could. It is a subject on which Cox is
discreetly silent. One or two things I have always had
in mind. First, that any objector would have to show
locus standi—that he had some "concern" in the matter
(the invitation is addressed "to all concerned"). This
requirement would, I think, be met by his showing that
he was either a parishioner, or a member of the
congregation, or even an adherent provided he had

registered as such. Otherwise I do not think he should be listened to. Secondly, that the objection must be to life or doctrine—it would certainly not be enough for the objector to claim that he couldn't abide the man's preaching, or that he thought him far too young for such a charge. Thirdly, that while the edict claims that the objection must be "immediately substantiated" it would be unreasonable to expect anyone to be in a position to produce full legal proof of an averment of, for example, heresy, or consistent drunkenness, at such a meeting. At the same time a mere averment of some discreditable conduct would not be adequate. But if a strong *prima facie* case were established then, as I see it, the Presbytery would have no option but to proceed in the matter. It would be essential that an opportunity be provided for the inductee to state whether or not he admitted the allegations. And, of course, he could not be expected to have come fully prepared to defend himself against them.

Assuming that a strong *prima facie* case has been presented, what then? First, I think the Presbytery would remit to some small body to investigate the matter with a view to reporting at a later time, and then would adjourn. Intimation would have to be made to the congregation that the Service was at least postponed, and this would be done in the most general terms. Throughout it should be kept in mind that it is very easy in such circumstances to wander into the field of defamation. It is clear that a *bona fide* objector can claim that he is fulfilling a public duty in that he has come forward in answer to an edictal invitation and that in consequence he enjoys a large measure of privilege. This would not avail him if it could be shown that he had been actuated by malice and that there was no probable cause for his complaint. But the Presbytery—and particularly its members as individuals—must walk warily, and, at this stage at least, it would seem wise to meet in private and to impress upon the members the supreme importance of observing confidentiality.

Introduction   When as a result of readjustment a new congregation has been formed of which the minister of one of the constituent parts has, in terms of the Basis, become minister it is customary for the Presbytery to arrange a Service of Introduction. Such a service is held also in any case where an appointment has been made on a terminable basis or to some office to which induction would be inappropriate. Introduction does not carry any legal consequences, and (unless ordination is also involved) no edict is served, although the person being introduced is expected to reaffirm the vows of his ordination and to sign the Formula.

Demission   The nature of the pastoral tie created by induction being the peculiar thing it is (as explained above), if for any reason a minister wishes to leave his charge he can do so only by applying to the Presbytery for leave to demit. "For any reason" includes retirement on account of age or of failing health, appointment to some other post whether or not under the jurisdiction of the Church, the desire to accept an invitation to a terminable appointment, the receipt of a Call from a charge abroad, or what have you—in fact, very literally "for any reason". The minister's letter asking leave to demit, indicating a date, and stating the grounds for the request, is laid on the table at the first meeting of Presbytery and it is resolved to deal with the matter at next meeting, the Clerk being instructed to cite parties, that is, the minister and the congregation, to that meeting for their respective interests.

Unless the reason for the minister's request is a very obvious one the Presbytery has a duty to appoint a small committee to confer with him. It is not unknown for circumstances—or members of a congregation— to get a man down so that in a mood of depression he feels he should just give it all up. In such circumstances it is most important that the Presbytery should be ready to adopt its pastoral role and take a firm hold of such a situation.

Should a minister take the law into his own hands and simply abscond then the Presbytery, after a lapse of forty days to allow of his return, is entitled to proceed against him in his absence on the ground of desertion and to depose him accordingly.

"Automatic Demission" There are two sets of circumstances in which demission is "automatic"— where a minister inducted subsequently to 1972 has attained the age of seventy, and where the terms of a Basis of Union or Linking or other form of readjustment includes a condition that the minister is to retire in the interest of readjustment. In the former case the Act specifically states that his ministry is "to terminate as if he had resigned his charge" and the Presbytery had fixed the date of his seventieth birthday for his demission. In the latter case it is understood that when the Presbytery agrees to the Basis of Union it agrees also to the demission which therefore takes place without further resolution on its part. It would, however, be most ungracious to allow what may often have been long and distinguished ministries to terminate in so off-hand a fashion. Even though the matter may carry no legal significance the Presbytery

will wish to have minister and representatives of the
congregation present at a convenient time so that the
occasion may be suitably marked.

Ius Devolutum There is a limit upon the time
allowed to a vacant congregation to call a minister.
From the date when they receive permission to call
(sometimes referred to as the *congé d'élire*) until the
minister has been inducted a total of six calendar
months is available. That, at least, is the letter of the
law, but in practice so long as a nominee has been
chosen within the six-month period no difficulty will be
raised. In any case, an extension of time can be applied
for, and—unless there be some compelling reason
against it—a further three months will be allowed
by the Presbytery. Even at that stage a further application can be made for extension, but some good
and sufficient reason will have to be advanced in
explanation of the delay. When it has been finally
determined that "time is up" the right and duty to
make an appointment falls to the Presbytery itself.
Even then an opportunity is given to the congregation
to hear the person nominated and to subscribe a call to
him. Thereafter induction follows the normal lines.

Visitation

Under this general heading of "visitation" I intend
to deal with two rather different ways in which a
Presbytery may be involved in the visitation of its
congregations—first the regular five-yearly visitation
of all congregations within the bounds, and secondly
the visitation which has to be organised when it is
reported that a certain congregation is believed to be in
an unsatisfactory state.

Quinquennial Visitation

Presbyteries are required by Act of General Assembly (XII, 1931, with amendments) to operate a system of Quinquennial Visitation whereby each congregation within the bounds shall receive a visit from a Committee of the Presbytery once within each period of five years. This, it should be noted, is not quite the same thing as once every fifth year. What Presbyteries have, in fact, to do is to arrange to cover all their charges within the first four years of each quinquennium, the fifth year being reserved for catching up on any which for some reason (such as vacancy, illness of the minister, involvement in readjustment, or the like) have not been dealt with in their regular place. The five-year periods began in 1931.

Object of Visitation It is laid down clearly in the Act that the object of the exercise is "to strengthen the hands of the minister, Kirk Session, office-bearers, and members, to advise them should anything appear to be unsatisfactory in the state of the congregation or not in accord with Church law and order, and in general to give counsel and encouragement as may be suitable to the circumstances of the case." In carrying out the visitation Presbyteries are urged "to keep particularly in view the promotion of the spiritual wellbeing of the congregation visited and the efficiency of the congregational agencies"—an exhortation repeated with rather wearisome regularity each year in the Deliverance of the Committee on General Administration.

Visiting Committee A special committee is appointed by the Presbytery in respect of each visitation due to be conducted. It should normally consist of two ministers and two elders and it is obviously desirable that the minister who is to act as Convener should be a person of some experience. The committee meets separately with minister, Kirk Session, and Finance Court (the minister being entitled to be present on each occasion), and on a convenient Sunday the Convener conducts the public worship of the congregation, expressing the interest and conveying the greetings and good wishes of the Presbytery. This is an important element in the exercise and one that should be taken seriously.

Questionnaire   A *pro forma* document has been prepared with lots of questions relevant to each of the three meetings. A considerable number of statistics are called for as well as a variety of particulars regarding finance, and it is therefore important that a copy be sent in advance so that those responsible may have these answers ready-to-hand in accurate form. Complaint is sometimes heard that the other questions are too "general". That they should be so is, I think, inevitable since what is in view is not so much to glean detailed information about the life of the congregation as to open up discussion in areas where difficulties and problems are needing to be aired, and where, if possible, help may be forthcoming in cases of need. Often you can learn far more from the attitude of a witness than you can from his answers. The wise and experienced quinquennial visitor will usually learn more from the atmosphere of the meetings than from anything that is entered on the schedule. Incidentally, the Convener of the Committee is provided in advance with a copy of the report from the previous quinquennium and is expected to satisfy himself that due attention has been paid to any recommendations made therein.

Advance Notice A copy of the completed report as that is to be submitted to the Presbytery has in each case to be sent timeously to the Kirk Session of the congregation visited, and the minister, Kirk Session, and any other party claiming an interest may appear at the Presbytery and be heard.

Synod Intervention The Act makes provision whereby the Presbytery is to report to the Synod any case where it is unable to express satisfaction with the condition of a congregation. The Synod is then to appoint a committee to make further enquiry in conjunction with the Presbytery. Failing satisfaction at this stage the matter is to be reported to the General Assembly through the General Administration Committee (now the Board of Practice and Procedure). The Act does not say so, but it is to be presumed that they too will appoint a committee to enquire. Unhappily the kind of unsatisfactory conditions that mar the life of many a congregation do not readily improve as a result of much visitation. Let it be that the buildings are in an appalling condition of disrepair, that there are no funds, that there is a complete want of leadership, and that all those in positions of responsibility have lost heart; or let it be that relations between minister and people are strained because of a general incompatibility that has built up over the years without anyone in particular being to blame. An infusion of funds in the one case, a change of ministry in the other, would doubtless work wonders: a lot of visiting and reporting is unlikely to help greatly.

In Private The Act requires that the Presbytery shall meet in private when any report on quinquennial visitation is given in. Oddly enough, no such provision is made when the matter comes before the Synod.

Trouble Brewing   One of the most promising possibilities of quinquennial visitation is that it should provide an early-warning system in cases where, for example, personal relations are becoming strained but have not yet completely broken down. The possibility of intervention at Presbytery level, if for no other purpose than to show interest and concern, ought to be of great value. Unhappily in practice it rarely seems to work that way. I vividly remember one case. I had reason to believe that all was not well in this congregation. No formal complaint had been lodged, but disturbing stories were reaching me. I was happy to note that they were due to be quinquennially visited, so I carefully hand-picked a strong committee and briefed the Convener on my fears and anxieties. At the meeting with the Kirk Session the Convener went out of his way to open up a free discussion—was there nothing else they would like to talk about, were there not any problems they might want to raise when they had the chance of the Presbytery representatives here? No, no problems! It was less than a month later that the lid blew off and we had a major situation on our hands. I suppose it's natural that in the best-regulated families you keep the skeletons carefully under lock and key when the neighbours are paying you a visit— and even more so when the police are around!

Altogether it must be conceded that the system of quinquennial visitation does not produce the results for which one might feel entitled to hope. It probably does a bit of good and provides some encouragement to those congregations which need it least, but it rarely seems to get through where help is most urgently and desperately required. It is not to be regarded on that account as a waste of time—which is far from being the case—and it should be carried through, by visitors and visited alike, with serious care and attention.

"Unsatisfactory State"

In terms of Act XXI 1960 there has been laid upon the Presbytery responsibility for taking action in any case when it comes to its knowledge, as a result of quinquennial visitation, on a petition from within the congregation, or on other good ground, that any congregation within its bounds "is considered not to be in a satisfactory condition". The first duty of the Presbytery is by visitation to ascertain the facts, and if satisfied that all is not well to attempt by counsel and consultation to set things right. If this fails the committee is to report to the Presbytery that there are grounds for believing that the trouble is substantially due to faults personal to the minister, or to the fault of named office-bearers or members. If the Presbytery accepts the report and agrees with its conclusions it is to arrange what is, in effect, a trial, with power, if the judgments are upheld, either to dissolve the pastoral tie and to declare the charge vacant, or to remove an office-bearer from office, or to issue a Certificate of Transference to a member, or even to suspend from Church membership, as the case may be and as justice appears to demand.

To the best of my knowledge only one case has ever been carried through to a conclusion under this legislation. The case had to do with a situation that had given cause for grave concern over a long period—indeed it could fairly have been said to have reached the proportions of a public scandal—and yet it was only after the most protracted negotiations that an issue was achieved. The Judicial Commission, as I remember, sat for at least a couple of full days, and yet it required a long session in the General Assembly before the Commission's unanimous recommendation that the pastoral tie should be severed was finally accepted.

Part of the trouble arises from the fact that when at length this kind of situation has officially reached the Presbytery in terms of the Act the time when "counsel and consultation" might have proved effective is long past. In any case, if they were the kind of people amenable to profit from counsel and consultation the mess would never have arisen in the first place! Further, the time when the blame can be laid squarely—or even "substantially"—at the door of one person or another has also passed. When misguided things are being done and provocative things are being said they have a way of attracting the same kind of things in retaliation, and the situation becomes too complicated to unravel. It is not just in the sphere of dynamics that the principle of action and reaction being equal and opposite applies. The sad aspect of the whole affair is that the Presbytery should have to stand by and see irreparable harm done to the cause of the Kirk and yet be powerless to intervene. It was a distinguished Procurator of an earlier day who expressed the view—off the record—that what we had here was really an Act in an unsatisfactory condition.

Records

Annual Inspection

Each congregation within the bounds is under obligation once a year to produce its records so that these may be inspected by, and attested in name of, the Presbytery. This is often referred to as the "Visitation of Records" although "inspection" seems a more accurate and less ominous term. The documents to be produced are the minute-books of Kirk Session and Financial Court, the Baptismal Register, the Communion Roll, the Roll of Baptised Persons not Communicants, the Property Register, and a certified copy of the previous year's Accounts.

Object of Examination   The Act of 1700 required that "a competent number of the fit and experienced ministers for that work" were to be appointed, and their task was to find whether there was anything to challenge, anything that appeared censurable in the actings of the court—that is to say, they were to concern themselves with the contents of the Kirk Session minutes (the Session being at that time the only court) and the object was to ensure that in all its dealings the Session had been acting legally and properly.

Today, I imagine, not overmuch heed is paid to this aspect of affairs, although, of course, if it is apparent that irregularities have been occurring this will not be allowed to pass without notice. The principal purpose, however, is to ensure that the records themselves are being properly engrossed and securely preserved. The points to which attention is usually directed are that all meetings should be shown as having been opened and closed with prayer, that all minutes should bear the signature of Moderator (or Chairman or Preses) and Clerk, that there are adequate rubrics or other device for quickly "spotting" a particular item of business, that corrections and alterations are adequately attested, that the full particulars are legibly entered in all registers, and that any matters to which attention has been drawn on a previous inspection have received proper attention.

Loose-Leaf Records   For many centuries the first requirement for any Church record was that it be contained in "a bound volume." The advantages flowing from this must be obvious, and in a day when people could be found who wrote beautiful copper-plate script and who enjoyed spending hours doing so, this was excellent and worked admirably. These days have passed and seem unlikely to return. The emergence of the typewriter has made it quick and simple to produce neat easily-read material—but not in a bound volume! A Regulation of Assembly of 1964 deals with this aspect of affairs. It accepts loose-leaf records subject to four conditions—first, that the pages be consecutively numbered as they come into use; secondly, that the last word on each page appear as the first word on the next; thirdly, that each page be initialled by the Moderator (in addition to his signature at the end); and, fourthly, that as soon as it is conveniently possible a suitable number of sheets be bound together into a volume. This, to all intents and purposes, is how Presbyteries have been keeping their records since long before the Regulation. The last requirement—about ultimate binding—is the one most likely to be defaulted on at congregational level, and it is the one that is not readily revealed at an annual inspection. Yet it is perhaps the most important of all. Great sheaves of loose papers in a cupboard in the house of the Session Clerk are—in the event of his sudden death, for example—liable to be swept away in some general clearance. This fate would not so easily overtake "a bound volume".

The Communion Roll   There is wide variety in the way Communion Rolls are kept. Here again, however, it is required that there be a bound volume showing a list of communicants with their dates and methods of joining, and, in due course, the dates and methods of their leaving. This can then be connected by some system of cross-reference with any type of card-index or loose-leaf method of keeping a record of attendances at Communion.

Roll of Baptised Persons not Communicants   It was on a deliverance of the Youth Committee in their report to the General Assembly of 1930 that it was resolved that Kirk Sessions should be required to maintain a Roll of Baptised Persons not Communicants and to produce this along with the other records at the annual inspection. Reference was made in the Report to the fact that this was a practice that had obtained in the U.F. Church. In that Church, in fact, the document had been called a "Roll of Young" and the law concerning it was in these terms: "All baptised young persons in the congregation, being members of the Church not in full communion, have special claims to supervision and care. Their names should be entered in a Roll kept by the Session; and each elder should endeavour to make himself acquainted with the young in his district, and to promote their spiritual welfare."

Here is enshrined an admirable idea, that of trying to maintain continuity of caring from the Cradle Roll through to the Communion Roll, particularly in the difficult period between leaving Sunday School and "reaching years of discretion", a period during which so many young people are lost to the Kirk. I think, however, that this is a matter where the emphasis must be laid upon what the District Elder can do by maintaining contact and manifesting interest rather than on the keeping of a Roll, however complete and up-to-date.

Undoubtedly a Roll can be of value and the law is that it has to be kept and annually produced.

Benefice Register

Under an Act of 1931 there is laid upon the Presbytery a duty which I strongly suspect is observed more in the breach than in the observance. This has to do with the maintaining and updating of a Benefice Register containing detailed information regarding the property of every charge within its bounds, particularly heritable property, funds held in trust, endowments for whatever purpose, valuable furnishings and equipment, objects of historical interest. The matter is of vast importance and a good register can be quite invaluable in supplying information as to the purpose and whereabouts of this and that and also sometimes in making it possible to dispel the quite erroneous but firmly held notions about possible destinations for interest on some trust fund.

I quote from Cox—"Every Presbytery must keep and annually revise a Benefice Register, containing all available information appertaining to every parish and chapel regarding the stipend and emoluments attached to the living, ecclesiastical property, trust funds, bequests, donations, mortifications, or charities, in which the minister or Kirk Session, or trustees or managers of quoad sacra parishes or chapels, have an interest or any right of administration; all relative writs, or registered copies thereof, to be produced if possible, and an inventory of them entered in the register with the names of their custodiers. The Presbytery is responsible for the accuracy of the register, and must therefore as far as possible verify information furnished to it." It is particularly important in relation to heritable property and trusts that there should be accurate information available and that this should include information regarding the custody of title deeds and of deeds of trust. I remember being informed in all seriousness by a Treasurer that there need be no difficulty in getting sight of their title deeds—"They're in a lawyer's office, I forget the exact name, but there's three bits to it—Somebody and Somebody and Somebody—and the office is in West Regent Street or is it West George Street, I'm no' right sure." It's easier if there's a Benefice Register.

In a Vacancy Again I quote from Cox—"During vacancies interim moderators of Kirk Sessions shall forthwith cause an inventory to be made of all Church properties which had been in the custody of the former minister, and have the said inventory carefully compared with the record in the Benefice Register of the Presbytery. On the admission of a minister to a charge, the inventory made on the occurrence of the vacancy shall be placed in his hands for the purpose of enabling him to ascertain that he has obtained the custody of all Church properties recorded therein, and within three months after his induction he shall report to the Convener of the Benefice Register Committee of the Presbytery, or to such other person as the Presbytery may designate, whether he has ascertained it to be correct or otherwise." Here too, I fear, these provisions are rarely fully—or even partially— complied with.

Keeping Up-to-Date   Part of the problem from the Presbytery Clerk's point of view arises from the requirement that the Register should be kept up to date. The obvious method of doing this is to submit to each congregation once a year a copy of the relevant pages and to ask them to mark up alterations. But a Presbytery Clerk once he has got a good record in his keeping is not readily going to part with it for any purpose whatever, for he knows from bitter experience the problem he may have in getting his hands on it again. Yet it is of considerable importance that each Presbytery should have a reliable inventory of all the property of the Kirk within its bounds.

Fabric

For the past twenty years or more the condition of the Church's property has been giving increasing cause for concern, and today the situation is fast assuming the proportions of a crisis. The middle of last century saw a great wave of Church building. After a century and a half the traditional Scottish stone building is liable to have come to be in need of extensive repair and renewal, not to say of continuing and unrelenting care. The acid that used to infuse the air of our industrial areas worked havoc with the stonework, while the dampness of the West of Scotland atmosphere encouraged dry-rot in the woodwork. Church Extension buildings put up between the wars and those erected in the last twenty years were all of them of necessity designed to meet a price, and, as is well known, the cheap job is rarely the most economical. The devotion to flat roofs has brought a host of

problems. Dry-rot infestation in properties both old
and young accounts each year for an enormous bill.
Building costs have risen very steeply in recent times.
And, to make matters worse, the upkeep of fabric is the
thing upon which, in a tight situation, it is easiest to
avoid spending money—you can put off till next year
what you haven't the cash to put in hand today. And,
even without inflation, we all know what kind of saving
that effects. So that, as I have said, the Church is
confronted with an outsize fabric problem, if not a
major crisis.

Within these same past twenty years a series of
"Acts anent the care of Ecclesiastical Property" have
sought to deal with the problem, or at least to prevent it
from getting out of hand. The only final solution if we
are to retain all our existing heritable property in
anything like a proper fashion is the creation of a truly
enormous fund from which grants can be made
available for a massive programme of repair and
upgrading. In my own view something on a scale
comparable to what Church Extension was forty years
ago is the least that will suffice. And alongside of that
there must go a merciless programme of pruning.
Properties that are no longer truly necessary in today's
situation must be sacrificed—for money spent on them
would simply be money down the drain—and we
surely don't have money to waste.

In the meantime the most strict observance of the
terms of the Act may help to secure for the future the
property that is still in reasonably good order.

Congregational Fabric Committee   The most recent of
the Acts was passed in 1979. It requires the
appointment in each congregation of a Fabric
Committee which shall contain, or shall co-opt, a

person with technical knowledge and experience. This Committee shall, at least once a year, carry out a thorough inspection of all the congregation's property (Church, Hall, Manse, etc) and it shall enter full particulars of the said inspection in a Property Register provided for the purpose, being at especial pains to record that recommendations arising from earlier inspections have been duly implemented, and if not why not. This Property Register is to be presented annually for the inspection of the Presbytery.

Presbytery Fabric Committee   The Presbytery in turn is to appoint a Fabric Committee including a person of technical know-how. Not only is this body to examine annually all congregational Property Registers, it is, at least once in each five-year period, to arrange an on-the-spot inspection of each congregation's property, and it is to carry out this inspection by itself or "by whatever agency it deems wise"—presumably a professional expert. When this Committee reports to the Presbytery with recommendations the congregational authority concerned shall have the right to be represented.

Insurance   The insurance of Church property is a matter of supreme importance today. A great many congregations are grossly under-insured, and this means that in the event, for example, of a fire which does considerable damage but does not involve complete destruction only a proportion of the loss actually incurred will be recoverable from the insurance—even although the total loss falls within the total sum insured. If you are only half-insured you can expect to be only half-compensated. In many cases this could put a congregation out of business. The plea is often made, "We simply cannot afford to insure."

There is a short answer to that one—"You simply cannot afford not to insure." The Act requires that the Presbytery Fabric Committee referred to above is to appoint a Sub-Committee on Insurance under the Convenership of "a person knowledgeable regarding insurance affecting buildings." This Sub-Committee is to be diligent in examining congregational Property Registers and, where appropriate, in offering advice in regard to insurance.

Readjustment

As was explained above when I was speaking about vacancies (page 38) simultaneously with the appointment of an interim moderator in a vacancy or anticipated vacancy the situation is reported to the Assembly's Church and Ministry Department, and its Unions and Readjustments Committee prepares, along with the Committee of the Presbytery, to consider the question so far as readjustment is concerned. The initiative lies with the Presbytery which has first to make up its mind whether in its view the question of readjustment should be pursued. If it thinks this is a case where that should not be done then it minutes a resolution to that effect giving the congregation permission to call a minister without restriction and it informs the Assembly's Committee accordingly. If the latter body does not concur then it has a power of veto and procedure in the vacancy will be sisted pending further exploration of the possibilities of the situation.

It is not my intention here to enlarge upon the various forms that readjustment may take—these are dealt with fairly fully in *A Guide to Congregational Affairs*—all

I want to do now is to trace the responsibility of the Presbytery in this department.

Investigation   The Presbytery appoints a committee (or its Readjustments Committee appoints a sub-committee) to conduct negotiations with the office-bearers of the vacant congregation and with those of any other with which it appears that some form of readjustment may be effected. It is not usual—and on balance I think it is not desirable—that the vacant congregation as such (still less any other congregation) should at this stage be brought into the discussions. It can, I know, be highly frustrating for good members to realise that things vitally affecting the future of their congregation "are going on behind their backs". At the same time it is surely reasonable to expect that members will trust their office-bearers to have the best interests of the congregation at heart and to accept an assurance that nothing will be finally and irrevocably decided without the approval of a duly called and constituted congregational meeting. There may be no harm in the office-bearers informing the congregation of the progress of the negotiations, but there is an old adage about who should see things "half-dune" and it is certainly my own view that, at what can be a rather delicate stage of negotiations, the less said the better.

If progress is achieved as a result of the Committee's labours and it appears that, say, a union of the congregation with one of its neighbours is a possibility, then a small group from each will meet jointly along with the Presbytery Committee to hammer out a Basis of Union (or of Linking or whatever it may be) setting forth the various conditions. This will then go back to each individual set of office-bearers for approval or adjustment—and so on until it has finally been got into a form which has the support of both.

Congregational Meetings By order of the Presbytery, meetings of the two congregations will be duly called "to consider, and if so advised to adopt, a Basis of Union". The proposed Basis should be stencilled or otherwise reproduced and copies distributed to members on the two Sundays when intimation of the congregational meeting is being given. It is not fair to hand them out during or immediately before the meeting itself—still less merely to read over the contents of the document. It is highly desirable that the two congregations should meet simultaneously, or, if that is not possible, that the one meeting should follow immediately upon the other. Untold harm can be done if opportunity is provided for gossip within one of the congregations about what happened and what was said at the meeting of the other—and even worse of what was alleged to have happened and to have been said.

These meetings are chaired by a member of the Presbytery who, after questions and discussion have been fully engaged in, has to put the question, "Is this congregation prepared to unite with the congregation of X in terms of this Basis of Union?" The votes should be counted even when unanimous. Voting is by standing up. There is no provision for any kind of referendum nor for absent members to record a vote. The Basis of Union cannot be amended—obviously both congregations must be accepting the identical document. If, however, the motion to unite is defeated it is in order—and could prove helpful—to agree a resolution that union would have been acceptable if Clause x of the Basis of Union had been amended to read, "......".

Judgment of Presbytery   The Presbytery has still to
reach a judgment on the matter, and this it will
normally do at the first ordinary meeting after the
congregations have met. If there is reason for haste the
Presbytery may actually have already approved the
proposed union "subject to acceptance by both
congregations of the Basis of Union." The fact that one
or both congregations have rejected the idea of union is
not an absolute bar to such union being effected,
though it will obviously be a very serious consideration
in the mind of the court when it reaches its decision.
So to this meeting of Presbytery the two or more
congregations are cited for their interest. They may be
heard, and, being at the bar, they are in a position, if so
advised, to appeal to the Synod against the judgment of
the Presbytery. Assuming, however, that agreement is
reached without appeal the matter is reported
to the Assembly's Committee whose concurrence is
necessary before the judgment can be put into effect.

Execution   In every case it is for the Presbytery to
effect the union or linking or whatever the case may be.
This is usually done by appointing an *in hunc effectum*
meeting when, at a special service in one of the
Churches involved, the congregations are declared to
be united (or linked) as from that date, and, if the
minister of one of the charges is to be minister of the
united (linked) charge then at the same service he is
"introduced" in that new capacity.

Terminable Tenure   Sometimes a congregation is
given permission to call a minister on the basis of a
terminable appointment. What that means, as the law
presently stands, is that the congregation is to be
served by a "minister without charge" whose tenure of
office may at any time be terminated by the Presbytery

on giving three months' notice to that effect. Such an arrangement is made, obviously, in a case where it is desired to link or unite the congregation with a neighbour but where that is not presently possible, the intention being that in due course two vacancies could be created simultaneously. The choice of such a minister is made as in a normal vacancy, but, once chosen, the minister, if he is in a charge has to demit that charge in order to be introduced to the terminable appointment—he is not "translated" as he would have been had he been inducted. It is of vital importance that a minute setting forth clearly the whole conditions of the appointment should be prepared, that a copy should be put into the hands of the appointee before he finally accepts and that he sign a paper in the Clerk's hands stating that he has seen, understands, and accepts the terms.

A dangerous element is frequently introduced— needlessly it seems to me—by specifying a time limit— "a terminable appointment for five years." This can easily be read as guaranteeing a minimum period of tenure and the person appointed may feel deeply aggrieved if at the end of two years he is told to go because a vacancy has now occurred in the other charge. "I was promised five years," he says in outraged tones, "I should never have come if I hadn't believed I was to be here for five years." When a period is mentioned, as in this case, it is meant to be a maximum—that the tenure may be terminated at any time and that the position will certainly be reviewed at the end of five years. My own conviction is that it is needless to mention a time at all—terminable means terminable, and it should be left at that.

If legislation at present before the Church goes through, such an appointment will in future be regarded as a charge, the appointee will be inducted, and if he is coming from another charge he will be translated. But the appointment will still be terminable on six months' notice from the Presbytery.

Dissolution Occasionally it happens that a congregation having, for some of the many reasons that bring heavy pressure today, reached the end of the road as an independent unit, and there being no other congregation with which it would be convenient, or agreeable, or realistic, for it to unite, it thinks it should simply bring its life-story to an end. If the Presbytery and the Assembly's Committee see this as a reasonable solution then it is for the Presbytery to take the necessary steps to petition the Synod to have the congregation dissolved.

Before this stage is reached, however, very specific arrangements should be made about the disposal of the physical assets of the congregation, including trusts and funds, and with particular reference to heritable property, and these should be incorporated in a Basis of Dissolution. If, for example, the buildings are vested in local office-bearers *ex officiis* it should be kept very sharply in mind that once the congregation has ceased to exist so have these gentlemen in the capacity in which they held the property, and that they will in consequence be unable to give a valid conveyance to a purchaser. It is good to have the heritable assets disposed of and a title given before the dissolution, but if this is not possible—as may often be the case—then the trustees holding the property *ex officiis* should execute a disposition conveying it to themselves as individuals (or to others nominated for the purpose by the congregation or the Presbytery) on the understanding that they are holding for the sole purpose of being able to give a title to an ultimate purchaser. The Basis of Dissolution should carefully and specifically provide for these and other similar matters.

The Presbytery must also see to it that the Basis of Dissolution makes arrangements for the oversight of the parish, at least on a temporary basis until a permanent reallocation of the area can be carried through. The destination of the moveable property should also be taken care of in the Basis. It may not be practicable to do this in full detail, but it is a good idea to have it put in the hands of a very small group of dependable people—it is so easy for this and that article—often of considerable value—to disappear as a "keepsake".

When all of these matters have received attention the Presbytery is in a position to proceed to the Synod with a petition. Once dissolution has been agreed upon by the members of the congregation there is often an understandable feeling that the sooner it takes place the better—let us go out on a reasonably triumphant note rather than just be allowed to drift away over a period of months. If, then, the timing of the Synod meeting is such as to involve delay, or if the disposal of the property necessitates a long period of waiting, there is nothing to prevent the Presbytery authorising the Kirk Session to discontinue public worship after the date on which they feel their story should be brought to a close. It would be necessary for the members of Kirk Session to leave their "lines" till the date of the official dissolution, but others would be free, and would be encouraged, to collect Certificates of Transference and lodge these elsewhere.

Transportation   It occasionally, but rarely, occurs that a congregation which has reached the end of its useful life in its present location is possessed of considerable funds, as the result of selling a valuable commercial site maybe. In such a case the congregation may feel there is something in their name and history that is worthy to be preserved and that they would be prepared to move to a new area of housing development where the presence of a Church would be desirable. This calls for transportation and is a matter very much within the province of the Presbytery. Where such transportations have taken place they have generally proved most successful. Grafting a new shoot on to an old root is a tried recipe for creating fresh life.

Finance

Apart from the collection of Presbytery and Assembly Dues already referred to (page 34) there are three points at which the Presbytery takes an interest in the financial affairs of each congregation—(1) in relation to its Annual Statement of Accounts, (2) in the matter of its payment of its minister, with all the various attendant outlays, and (3) in connection with its contribution to the Mission and Service Fund.

Annual Congregational Accounts

A certified copy of the Annual Statement of Accounts has to be lodged with the Presbytery at the time of the annual inspection of records (page 55). The Model Deed of Constitution for Parishes *quoad sacra*

1965 (under which most of our present-day congregations operate) stipulates that the "said accounts shall, after submission to and approval by the congregation, be laid before the Presbytery within one month thereafter, for examination and attestation to the effect that the accounts are correct and are in accordance with the terms of this Constitution." Even those congregations which operate under a different constitution are under obligation to make available for inspection a certified copy of their accounts. Apart from satisfying itself as to the regularity of the financial transactions recorded therein, the Presbytery has sometimes to make financial assessments upon congregations and can do so fairly only in the light of the information supplied in the accounts.

A model type of congregational account has been prepared by the General Finance Committee of the Assembly, and its adoption by all congregations is recommended, but not obligatory. It would certainly be a great convenience if some measure of uniformity could take the place of the welter of different types of accounting presently in use. It must at the same time be recognised that we are wholly dependent here on the dedicated service of volunteers and we have to accommodate to the kind of accounting to which they are accustomed.

Maintenance of the Ministry

The Fund for the Maintenance of the Ministry is one whose roots lie deep and whose influence spreads wide. I think it is worth while to take a very cursory glance at the historical picture—which is, in fact, a series of pictures. Only from some understanding of how it all came about can the rather peculiar pattern be fully understood. A word, then, about four separate traditions.

The Old Parishes   It would be far beyond the scope of this work to trace the history of stipend in the old Church of Scotland. Let it be said simply that from the days of the Reformation the Kirk in Scotland was supported by a tax on the fruits of the soil—teind, a survival of the tithes imposed by Moses. Stipend was not a salary but a "living" and it vested in the minister in virtue of his having been inducted and being in occupation of the charge on Michaelmas Day in any particular year. For long it was payable, literally and exclusively, in the form of victual—that is to say, so many bolls of bear (barley), so many firkins of meal, and so on. It was as comparatively recently as 1808 that an Act of Parliament introduced machinery whereby these obligations could be converted into sums of money, by the use of the "Fiars' Prices" which determined the price of the various grains each year in each county. Then in 1925, in preparation for the Union of 1929, a further Act of Parliament provided for stipend to be "standardised"—fixed at a constant figure instead of fluctuating with the price of the various commodities. All of the old parishes derived their stipends from teinds, and after 1925 it was paid not to the ministers but to the General Trustees in the form of standardised stipend and was remitted by them to the Maintenance of the Ministry Committee whose responsibility it was to determine how it was to be allocated among the congregations in the former parish—the area within which it was collected, the "area of preference".

The effect of inflation generally has been so to devalue the ancient patrimony of the Church that today it provides the merest fraction of the Church's stipend requirements. Had stipend still been tied to the price of grain an old parish whose income from teind is now fixed at say £500 would have had at its disposal perhaps twenty times that sum, that is to say a figure of £10,000.

The quoad sacras With the enormous movement of population and the increase in urbanisation consequent upon the Industrial Revolution new parishes had to be erected in many places, and obviously there was no way of making any of these a charge on the fruits of the soil—there was now considerably less soil left to support those already there. A few expedients were resorted to—the emergence of the "Burgh Churches" for instance, where resources had to be found by the burghs for the provision of stipend in the new parishes (three charges in Paisley had their stipend assured for them in terms of a River Cart Navigation Act!). Then a fund was introduced to which the Church as a whole was asked to contribute to provide the most modest of income for the ministers of the "smaller livings"—many of them small indeed!

Before a new cause could be erected into a parish *quoad sacra*, endowments had to be made available sufficient to provide a stipend of not less than £120 per annum. It was further required that these be in the form of feu-duties and ground-annuals—the gilt-edged securities of that day. With the steady deterioration in modern times of tenement properties in our cities a great many of these endowments have in our day become utterly worthless. Here again the patrimony made available by the generosity of an earlier generation has slipped from us.

The U.P.s   When the Churches of the Secession and
of the Relief united in 1847 to form the United
Presbyterian Church they had between them just over
five hundred congregations. In their early days these
congregations must have faced a quite terrifying
financial situation, for suddenly they had to find the
wherewithal to build a Church and a Manse and to
provide a stipend—and in the establishment they had
gained no experience whatever of that kind of giving.
That they should have been able to meet this challenge
produced not only a justifiable sense of pride in their
achievement but also a feeling of bitterness against
everything connected with the State whose interference
with the affairs of the Kirk had in their view driven
them out into this wilderness. Hence a quite belligerent
"voluntaryism". Hence too a tradition that the U.P.
Churches paid their own ministers, paid them what
they thought they deserved, and bitterly resented any
attempt at interference. In the Kirk traditions die
hard. At the Union of 1929 there were one or two
former charges of this persuasion who agreed to come
in only on a written assurance that they would not at
any time be asked to accept any of the money that had
its origin in teind.

In the early days of the U.P. Kirk assistance was
given in small sums by the Home Mission Board to
augment stipends in the most urgent cases. Until in
1868 it was resolved to open an Augmentation Fund
which was run on lines not dissimilar to the
Sustentation Fund which by that time was an
established feature of the life of the Free Church.

The Frees   At the Disruption of 1843 when the Free
Church came into being some 450 ministers left the
establishment—which meant, of course, that they left

the security of manse, glebe, stipend. This must have presented Dr Chalmers and the other leaders of the movement with a problem of breathtaking magnitude. To these brave men and their families they owed an enormous responsibility. The answer to the question as to how all these people were to be supported was found in the creation in the new Church of a Sustentation Fund. Out of this central pool each minister was paid an "equal dividend" which, it was expected, would wherever possible be supplemented by a direct payment from his own congregation.

The U.F.s For some time after the union of the U.P and the Free Churches in 1900 the Sustentation and the Augmentation Funds of the two bodies continued to function side by side. Later, however, the Central Fund was inaugurated, whereby out of a central pool any minister whose total income was less than £200 received graduated payments. A further revision of these regulations in 1920 led to the emergence of a Minimum Stipend Fund based on essentially the same principles as those with which we are familiar today.

Post-1929 Since the union of the Churches in 1929 the Minimum Stipend Fund has operated on the basis that, no matter what his own congregation is able to pay him, a minister of a charge will in any year receive not less than the amount of the Minimum Stipend that has been determined for that year. The attempt was made some time ago to introduce Seniority Payments and Family Allowances, but these had a very short life indeed. Those congregations which are in a position to do so give Aid to the Fund, those unable out of their own resources to pay the Minimum Stipend receive Aid from the Fund. The Minimum Stipend is, of course, a minimum, and those congregations able to do so are expected to pay stipends in excess of that figure. Proposals for a flat level of stipend for all ministers have from time to time been advanced but have never gained wide support from the side either of ministers or of congregations.

In the early days we had to wait till about February to see how much cash was in the Fund before the Minimum Stipend for the previous year could be struck, and ministers on the Fund received payment some time thereafter. The situation has now been reached where the amount of the Minimum Stipend for the following year is declared at each General Assembly. It should be noted that it is "declared" by the Committee and that the General Assembly "learns" of it "with interest"—it is not determined by the General Assembly and a motion at the Assembly that, for example, it be fixed at a different figure would be an incompetent one.

Vacancy Schedule   Stipend arrangements affecting a ministry are determined during the vacancy. Once it has been agreed that a congregation is to be allowed to call a minister, a Vacancy Schedule is sent from the Assembly's Maintenance of the Ministry Committee and a meeting is arranged of the Financial Court at which representatives of the Presbytery attend to assist with the completion of the Schedule. It used to be that each case was an *ad hoc* exercise, but thanks to the genius of the late Karl Greenlaw there was devised a system of "Appropriate Stipends and Aid to the Fund". The object of this is that for every congregation in the Church there is a figure for the stipend it should be expected to pay and for the aid it should be expected to contribute or should be entitled to receive; and unless for very special cause these are the figures that have to be entered in the Vacancy Schedule. The Schedule indicates also the sources from which the stipend is derived, whether there is a manse, what provision is made for travelling and for the payment of listed expenses.

Appropriate stipends are fixed by the Presbytery with concurrence of the Assembly's Committee. Individual Vacancy Schedules have, of course, to originate at congregational level and require the imprimatur of the local Financial Court as well as of the Presbytery and of the Assembly's Committee.

Payment of Stipend For some years now all payments of stipend have been made through the Edinburgh offices and are paid directly into the minister's bank account each month. In this day of pay-as-you-earn, national insurance contributions and pension payments, there are many advantages in such a system. One of these is that it helps to avoid the danger of it appearing that the minister is in the pay (and in the employ) of the congregation. To make it possible to operate, of course, it is necessary for local treasurers to advance monthly transmissions of the sums due by them towards stipend, aid, and pension, and to do so timeously. Gone, mercifully, are the days when the minister of a *quoad omnia* parish could be twelve months or longer in his post without having received a penny of stipend—I myself had to survive for nine months on an advance *ex gratia* of £100.

An induction to a vacant charge cannot be held until a Vacancy Schedule has been duly approved by all concerned, and it is required that immediately after the induction the Presbytery Clerk shall put into the hands of the new minister an extract minute of the Assembly's Maintenance of the Ministry Committee setting forth

the financial arrangements that are to obtain during
his ministry.

Revision Schedule   Should circumstances arise within
a congregation in consequence of which the figures
agreed as appropriate are no longer so because the
general financial situation of the congregation has
improved (or more likely has deteriorated) to a
material extent, then the congregation concerned can
apply to the Presbytery for the issue of a Revision
Schedule, and this request will be passed to the
Assembly's Committee which will issue such a
schedule. This will be dealt with in the same way as the
original Vacancy Schedule, and once agreed will
become the basis of the congregation's responsibility in
this field.

It must be apparent, therefore, that although a
minister is inducted in all good faith on the strength of
the figures approved in the Vacancy Schedule he is not
guaranteed that income for the duration of his
incumbency—the guarantee covers the payment of the
current Minimum Stipend, but beyond that it does not
stretch.

Mission and Service

Our early forefathers in the Kirk knew nothing
about the "Schemes of the Church" and mighty little
about giving for "others"—indeed very little about
giving at all. The only collection, taken quite often at
the kirk-door or at the kirkyard-gate, was for the
support of the poor of the parish and was itself of the
most modest proportions. The tale of the man who
wanted "change of a penny for the plate" is not at all
apocryphal, as witness the following quotation from
the First Statistical Account (1793) where one parish

minister somewhat bitterly records that "the number of the old and infirm at present on the list amounts to 32 persons while the annual collections come to no more than 42/6½ stg. In this large treasure there were one shilling, five sixpences, 443 pennies and 50 farthings."

Schemes of the Church When, however, in course of last century the Church became increasingly conscious of its obligations in many fields far beyond the bounds of the parish, far indeed beyond Scotland itself, opportunity had to be provided for members to subscribe towards these objectives — Foreign Missions, Highlands and Islands, Jewish Missions, Aged and Infirm Ministers' Fund, and so on. This was done by "uplifting special collections" — often by a plate presented at the Church door on leaving. It is easy to see how these came to be known as "retiring collections" — it was John White who remarked that they were often "very retiring". As the pressure increased the General Assembly intervened to the extent that each year they appointed the Sundays (rather more than one a month) when each of the Schemes in turn was to be beneficiary of the retiring offering.

Soon the membership as a whole rather revolted against this haphazard method. The complaints of the Committees concerned were even louder. The income of an important Committee, they claimed, could be halved if its collection fell to be taken on a disastrously wet Sunday. Besides, the system took no account of the vastly different budgets of the various Committees. It was a system characterised by a complete lack of anything that could be called systematic.

W.F.O. Early in the present century there emerged the Weekly Freewill Offering system. It was not to be

wondered at that a system so business-like and
generally efficient should have evoked criticism in the
early stages—anything which looks like imposing an
element of the systematic on a Kirk activity is liable to
be seen in some quarters as a threat to the free
movement of the Spirit! It was not long, though, till the
advantages of the scheme came to be appreciated and
the system itself has come to be all but universally
accepted.

At first the envelope made provision whereby the
subscriber could say how much of the contents was
"for ourselves" and how much was "for others".
People grew careless in this regard and in any case a lot
of book work was involved. So it came about that it was
left largely to the Financial Court to determine how
much was needed at home, how much should go to
schemes generally, and in what proportion it should
be divided out amongst them. To assist with this
the Assembly each year sent out a breakdown of the
£1 in the proportion of the Committee budgets and
many courts in their allocating followed this fairly
scrupulously. But there were those who for one reason
or another had a particular attachment to a "pet
scheme" and insisted on giving more generously to this
than to others. Came the day when the Committees
were unashamedly competing for an increasing "share
of the cake" and congregations were besieged with
special appeals, targets, partnership plans, and what
have you. The whole affair was getting completely out
of hand.

Co-ordinated Appeal   It was the General Assembly of
1959 that placed on the statute-book an Act anent a
Co-ordinated Appeal to Congregations for the Support
of the Work of the Church though 1st January 1961

was the operative date for its inception. The first object of this new plan was to substitute one co-ordinated appeal in place of the multitude of competing appeals that had been becoming increasingly self-defeating. At first it had been envisaged that the claims of the Maintenance of the Ministry would be included on all fours with those of the other schemes, but in the end it had to be agreed that Maintenance of the Ministry and Aged and Infirm Ministers' Fund should remain outwith the general appeal with a right to continue as in the past to reach their own arrangements with congregations. This, although conceded at the time, was felt to be unfortunate, and attempts have been made throughout the intervening years to bring the claims of Church and Ministry under the umbrella. A greater measure of co-operation has now been achieved and there, as I see it, it must rest for in the nature of things it is difficult to get around the fact that a congregation's obligation to support its own minister is in a different case altogether from, for example, its responsibility for the support of Social Service.

A second object of the Appeal was to provide at Assembly level some measure of control over the spending of the various committees, by indicating to them in advance the kind of budget within which they would have to operate, and by ensuring that, unless they could be assured of the necessary funds, they would not light-heartedly launch out into new fields, no matter how compelling the challenge might appear.

S. and B. Committee The Stewardship and Budget Committee was created to take charge of this work, and after a number of years the name "Mission and Service" was substituted in place of what was felt to be the none too poetic "Co-ordinated Appeal". Unhappily the new name does not itself rise to any dizzy height of imaginative challenge, and while the new set-up has been remarkably successful in producing the money it hasn't noticeably engendered within the Church any burning enthusiasm for the work which the money makes possible.

The *modus operandi* today is that each spending committee submits a budget for the coming year and this is inspected with minute care, and where appropriate pruned, by the Stewardship and Budget Committee which then adds all the various sums together and so arrives at a global total for the coming year's requirements. To this a figure is added in respect of "contingencies"—though in practice the principal contingency appears to be a shortfall on the amount asked. The total thus reached is now divided according to a formula that brings out an amount expected from each congregation of the Kirk. Until recently the division was among the Presbyteries and they had then the duty of dividing up among congregations. Now the Presbytery has the duty first of adjusting the allocations if the circumstances known to it seem to demand this, and secondly of "selling" the figures to the congregations—not always an easy task.

Mission and Service Fund   It was inevitable that some such scheme should be devised, and, within its limitations, the Mission and Service Fund works admirably. It suffers, as I see it, from two great disadvantages inseparable from any system based on a principle of co-ordination. For one thing it can all too easily be seen as a kind of tax, for it takes the subscriber a stage farther away from the objective of his generosity. A missionary in the pulpit on the day when the retiring collection was for Foreign Missions could—if he was "on the ball" and it wasn't raining too heavily—fairly bring in the cash. Whereas it is difficult to work up enthusiasm for contributing to a Co-ordinated Appeal—it's like asking you to feel a glow of satisfaction as you see how much pay-as-you-earn has been deducted from your salary! There used to be congregations which would genuinely stretch themselves till it really hurt to maintain their givings to Foreign Missions; you just cannot expect the same dedication and sense of devotion to the demands of the Mission and Service Fund. The other weakness is that, human nature being what it is, Congregation A, instead of thrilling to the challenge of finding £2,000 for the Mission and Service Fund, is much more likely to complain bitterly about being asked for so much when Congregation B just round the corner is "getting away with £1,200".

The Presbytery has a duty to convince congregations of the reasonableness of the sum they are asked to contribute, and, if they fall significantly short, to discover what is amiss and seek to remedy it.

Board of Stewardship and Finance It seems almost certain that there is shortly to emerge under the Assembly Council's scheme of administrative reorganisation a Board of Stewardship and Finance which will unite the Stewardship and Budget Committee with the General Finance Committee and which will have a remit to cover the promotion of teaching and understanding of Christian Stewardship among members, the provision of programmes to assist congregations in promoting Christian giving, responsibility for the preparation of a Co-ordinated Budget to meet the costs of ministry (active and retired), of Mission and Service and of General Purposes, and

for bringing this budget to the Assembly for approval.
This new degree of co-ordination promises to be
interesting.

Worship

The claim is frequently heard that the minister alone
is in sole and absolute charge of the worship of his
congregation. This is true in the limited sense that
no-one else in the congregation has any responsibility
for the conduct of worship, but beyond that it is a
dangerously misleading statement. The true position
is that the Presbytery is responsible for worship
throughout its congregations and that in the exercise of
this responsibility it adopts the parish minister as its
executive officer. Clearly this does not invest the
minister with any absolute authority, and in particular
he may at any time be called upon by the Presbytery to
render an account of his activities in this field.

Innovations in Worship In 1866 the General Assembly interpreted the relevant section of the Act of
Parliament of 1592 as follows—"It belongs to the
Presbytery to regulate matters concerning the performance of public worship and the administration of
ordinances, in accordance with the laws and settled
usages of the Church; and they are to take cognisance
of the alleged existence or proposed introduction of any
innovation or novel practice coming regularly to their
notice, and after inquiry, if this appears necessary, are
to give such deliverance as seems to be warranted by
the circumstances of the case and the laws and usages
of the Church; and it is their duty to enjoin the
discontinuance or prohibit the introduction of any
novel practice inconsistent with the laws and settled

usages of the Church, or a cause of division in the congregation, or unfit for any cause to be used in the worship of God, either in general or in the particular kirk." These are strong words! Any member of a congregation is entitled at any time to petition the Presbytery craving that it will exercise its powers under this statute.

Who May Conduct   The law is perfectly clear that the authority to conduct public worship can be conferred only within a limited group of people—ministers, probationers, deaconesses licensed to preach, students for the ministry or for the licensed diaconate, lay missionaries, readers, and auxiliary ministers. It is not unusual today for a service on some special occasion to be conducted by a group of elders, or of members of the Woman's Guild, or by the Youth Fellowship. The legality of this is, I think, rather doubtful. It seems clear that if such a service is to be held then at the least the minister himself must be present and be nominally in charge of the proceedings. If anything is done amiss it is he and not the perpetrator who will be answerable to the Presbytery.

Who May Celebrate   When a parish minister is arranging a summer exchange with an American counterpart, for example, he should officially apply to the Presbytery for leave of absence, and, if it is intended that the visitor will be available to administer baptism or to dispense the sacrament of the Lord's Supper, the minister should at the same stage ask the Presbytery to grant authority to the visitor to celebrate the sacraments. If the conduct of marriages is involved the local Registrar should be informed. The minister himself cannot authorise a minister of another denomination to dispense the sacraments even although it is in his own parish. A minister of another denomination whose orders are recognised by the Church of Scotland may on occasion be invited to dispense either of the sacraments, but the fact must be reported in writing to the Presbytery Clerk within fourteen days of the event.

General Oversight

Presbyteries have an overall duty of supervision in all matters affecting the spiritual well-being of the Church and of its members within their bounds. While jealously guarding the privileges of Kirk Sessions and of members, the Presbytery has a right (and a duty) to intervene at least to the extent of giving counsel and admonition when it thinks this may prove helpful. A delicate hand is needed to guide the Presbytery here if it is to steer a middle course between on the one hand becoming an interfering busybody and on the other remaining an ivory-tower spectator of disharmony, error, and trouble.

Erection of New Parish   I include under the general heading of oversight the power of the Presbytery to initiate procedure towards the creation of a new charge, though, of course, it is for the General Assembly on petition to pass the necessary Act and for the Delegation of Assembly to grant the appropriate constitution. There is not today the dramatic movement of population that had characterised practically the entire period since the end of the First World War. Indeed the movement today seems to be towards the rehabilitation of the run-down areas in the centres of our towns and cities. But should the need arise—where, say, a new town is being started from scratch—it is for the Presbytery to take the initiative towards having a Church Extension charge set down wherever it is believed to be needed.

Public Affairs This may also be as good a place as any to interject a brief paragraph in regard to the position of Presbyteries in relation to matters of public concern within their bounds. Often when some question has arisen with implications narrowly affecting the Church the matter may be one of wider than local concern, and in such a case the wise policy may well be for the Presbytery either to overture the General Assembly (see page 150) to have the matter dealt with at national level, or, alternatively, to approach the Church and Nation Committee to see whether the issue can be brought to the Assembly as an item in their report.

If, on the other hand, the matter is one of purely local concern then the wise course may well be for the Presbytery to throw in its weight behind the Kirk Session of the area affected—there are many affairs where the local Kirk Session has an official standing when the Presbytery has none.

5

What It Works At

SUPERVISING MINISTERS AND OTHERS

The Presbytery has oversight of a wide variety of people, all of them in some way in the service of the Church, though not necessarily in the employment of any of its congregations or committees—Ministers, Students for the Ministry, Probationers and Licentiates, Lay Missionaries, Members of the Diaconate, Readers, Auxiliary Ministers—all come under supervision of some Presbytery of the Church. The nature of the relationship varies from one class to the next, so we shall look at them one at a time.

Ministers

Ministers who are members of a Presbytery come under the supervision of that Presbytery. Those who are ministers of parishes are answerable to the Presbytery for the conduct of their duties as well as for their life and doctrine, those in the full-time service of the Church may in relation to their work be answerable to some committee or congregation which engages and pays them, but for life and doctrine it is to the Presbytery they must answer. Others, such as teachers of religious education with or without Presbytery seats, are under direction and control of an Education

Authority, but in respect of doctrine and conduct they are answerable to the Presbytery. This does not mean that the court has any power to dismiss a teacher from his post, but it does have the power—and, it may be, the duty—to deprive him of his status as a minister. The Presbytery, that is to say, is in no position to prevent heresy being taught in a school, but it can ensure it is not being taught by one of its own ministers.

I remember a number of years ago an argument that developed between the then Principal Clerk of Assembly and the then Principal of Glasgow University regarding the appointment of a Professor within the Faculty of Divinity. To qualify for his seat in Presbytery the Professor was required to reaffirm the vows of his ordination and to sign the Formula. The Principal expressed the strongest resentment of this, claiming that it meant "imposing a test on my chair". This view resulted, surely, from a confusion between the "chair" and the "seat". We in the Church had neither the desire nor the power to impose conditions on the appointment of a professor, but if the appointee was a minister of the Church of Scotland the Presbytery and the Presbytery alone had the right to say on what conditions he should retain his status as a minister and his seat in the Presbytery.

Ministers Without Charge If a minister relinquishes his charge in order to take up an appointment outwith the Church and for which his ministerial status is an irrelevance—as a teacher of mathematics, a journalist, a social worker, a solicitor—he will normally retain his status as a minister but he will lose his seat in Presbytery. Unless he has voluntarily relinquished his status he is required to lodge a Presbyterial Certificate

with the Presbytery within whose bounds he has come
to reside, and he then comes under the supervision of
that Presbytery. (But see what is written in regard to
Presbyterial Certificates hereunder—page 92.) People
sometimes imagine that a minister who has no longer a
seat in Presbytery ceases to be subject to the
Presbytery. That is not the case. So long as he
continues to hold the status of a minister of the Church
a person must be under the care of and answerable to
one of its Presbyteries. Should a minister leave the
service of the Church of Scotland to enter that of
another denomination he will cease to be under
Presbyterial care, but he should be given a Presbyterial
Certificate, and this he should lodge with the
responsible authority in his new denomination. Once
this has been done he has ceased to be a minister of the
Church of Scotland.

A Probationer who has been ordained—say as an
Assistant in a Parish—and who thereafter leaves the
service of the Church of Scotland becomes a Minister
without Charge.

Certificate of Status   An interesting situation arises
when a minister who has gone to work with another
denomination wishes to return to the service of the
Church of Scotland. Such a man applies to the
Committee on Probationers and Transference and
Admission of Ministers for a Certificate of Eligibility,
and this entitles him to be elected in a vacancy. It is,
however, only when he is inducted to a charge or
confirmed in an appointment that he once again
acquires the status of a Minister of the Church of
Scotland—in the interim he is still under the discipline
of the Church he is intending to leave, the Church
which he probably thinks he has already left. This is

not at all a satisfactory situation. The Church he is leaving are unlikely to be much interested in him, and since he has left their territory they are ill-placed to exercise jurisdiction. Suppose a *fama clamosa* were to arise concerning such a minister, the Committee which had issued the Certificate of Eligibility would, presumably, withdraw it, and would be entitled to do so. But if what had happened was that someone had laid a complaint charging some grave moral or doctrinal fault—what then? The Committee has no authority whatever to put the minister on trial, and he is not under the jurisdiction of any Presbytery which alone could begin a libel process. The only remedy available to the complainer would seem to be to await his election to a charge and then to appear as an objector—far from a satisfactory solution.

Demission of Status It is an interesting fact that while the law makes provision for a minister to be deprived of his status it has nothing at all to say about how he may of his own volition relinquish that status. The late James Longmuir had an interesting theory about the reason for this which I think may well provide the explanation. It was his view that in the opinion of our fathers the sanctity of the ministerial calling was such that for a man so much as to contemplate relinquishing his ministry was for him to be guilty of a sin so grievous that he deserved to be deprived of it! He was not allowed to discard his status, he was stripped of it. At the present day, I imagine, if a minister indicates a desire for any reason to discontinue being a minister he will intimate accordingly to the Presbytery which will doubtless confer with him in relation to the gravity of the step he is taking, but if it finds he is clear in his intention it will accept his demission of status, informing the Church and Ministry Department accordingly. There will, of course, be no question of the granting of a Certificate in such a case.

In this context it is of interest to note that under civil law a minister of the Church of Scotland is barred from becoming a Member of the House of Commons. Indeed the situation is worse in that before he can become a candidate in a Parliamentary election a minister of the Kirk has not only to demit his parish but has also to relinquish his status as a minister. The only case of this kind which, within my personal knowledge, has come to an actual issue was about thirty years ago when the Presbytery of Paisley with very great reluctance accepted the demission of status of one of its younger ministers. In the event he was unsuccessful at the election and could perfectly well have continued in his parish—had he still been a minister. In fact he secured an appointment in a political organisation—but a good minister was lost to the Kirk. I understand that Parliament itself is looking at this issue at the present time and we can only hope that something may be done to remove what appears an unfair disqualification, particularly as it affects only ministers of the Established Church and priests of the Roman Catholic Church.

Presbyterial Certificate   Act I of 1976 provides that a minister, on demitting his charge to take up an appointment which involves relinquishing his seat in Presbytery, shall be issued with a Presbyterial Certificate which shall be valid until 30th June next and which may be renewed annually thereafter. Unless he holds such a certificate he shall not be at liberty to exercise any of the functions of the ministry. This without prejudice to his status as a minister.

Application for the renewal of the certificate is to be made to the Clerk of the Presbytery to which the minister is subject not later than 30th April in any year, and such application is to give details of present employment and of ministerial functions exercised in course of the previous year. If the certificate is allowed to lapse it may be renewed on application to the Presbytery, but it will not become effective till 30th June following.

The Act does not define what constitute "the functions of the ministry". It could be argued that only those activities are struck at which belong exclusively to the ordained ministry—celebration of the sacraments, conduct of marriages, blessing the people. It seems to be generally accepted, however, that the conduct of public worship is included, and that, unless he holds a current certificate, such a minister is barred from accepting pulpit supply.

This Act of 1976 appears to have created a gap in the law. It specifically repeals the earlier legislation which was contained in Act XV of 1935. This had provided for the issuing of a Presbyterial Certificate which confined itself to vouching for the minister's good standing—that his character and conduct were in all respects becoming his profession—and he took this with him when he moved from one Presbytery to another. Once this certificate had been lodged and he had been welcomed into his new Presbytery the document itself lost all significance and could be destroyed. It was in all respects comparable to the "lines" which enable a member to move from one congregation to another. This type of Presbyterial Certificate would seem to have been replaced by the new document which might more properly be called a

Practising Certificate. But what of the minister outwith
the service of the Church who has no desire to perform
the functions of the ministry and who deliberately
allows this practising certificate to lapse? So long as he
stays put his Presbytery continues to have him under
its care and all is well. But if he decides to move, what
then? He doesn't have a practising certificate since he
never needed such a thing, and he cannot get one till
the end of next June at earliest; and he cannot get a
Presbyterial Certificate of the old sort since there is no
longer such a thing. There should surely be some way
to enable the Presbytery which such a man is leaving to
vouch for his character and conduct.

Discipline

As has been said, all ministers, whether or not they
are ministers of charges, are subject to the Presbytery
in the matters of life and doctrine. Any attempt to
enlarge on this subject brings us into the difficult realm
of discipline. I shall confine myself to a fairly general
treatment of a highly complicated theme.

One preliminary observation which I should like to
make has to do with the position of the Presbytery
Clerk when resort has to be had to the machinery of
discipline. If any breath of scandal affecting one of its
ministers comes to the knowledge of a Presbytery—
and for practical purposes this means to the ear of the
Presbytery Clerk—that official will probably take steps
to discover exactly what is amiss and whether there is
anything he can do "off the record" to put things right.
This is both understandable and commendable, but in
an area where the greatest caution has to be observed
the Clerk must move with much discretion. In
particular he has to keep constantly in mind that he

may not be successful in his efforts and that the issue may well develop into a full-scale libel case in which he is expected to act as prosecutor for the Presbytery, or at the very least that he will have much to do with the preparation of the case. It would be most unfortunate if the unhappy minister concerned had been encouraged to weep on the shoulder of the Clerk to the extent of making an incriminating confession to him in his capacity as the "friend of the accused". A Presbytery Clerk could find himself in a most embarrassing situation if called to give evidence regarding such an interchange.

The last thing I should want to recommend in this kind of situation is a cold, legalistic approach. At the same time I have always taken the view that there are only two ways of acting in such a case—the legal way and the illegal way—and I've always had a strong preference for the former. I should go so far as to say it is wise to proceed in a situation of this kind with a picture in one's mind of the matter ending up by being appealed to the General Assembly, and of finding oneself standing there at the bar defending the Presbytery for its conduct of the affair. The best-intentioned efforts to help can so easily be represented as unauthorised interference. This is an area where the Clerk should advance carefully, with caution in mind and Cox in hand.

Instituting Proceedings The Act (of 1935) underlines the need for the utmost caution in instituting proceedings against a minister or licentiate, and requires that ere this be done a complaint shall have been lodged either in a writing subscribed by the complainer or in a statement made by him in presence of the Presbytery, in either case along with some account of its probability. It may be, of course, that there is a *fama clamosa* (a public scandal) of such intensity that the Presbytery for its own vindication feels bound to take the initiative and institute an action even in the absence of an accuser. The wise course at this stage would seem to be to remit the affair to a very small select committee which should, if possible, include someone with legal experience. The first duty of such a committee is to conduct a preliminary enquiry.

Preliminary Enquiry The accused person shall be informed of the arrangements for the preliminary enquiry and shall have the right to be present throughout the course of it and shall have full opportunity of defending himself thereat. He may be represented at such enquiry by a solicitor or other agent. It has to be kept clearly in mind that this is not a trial, but only an enquiry to establish (a) that there are grounds to believe that there may be guilt, and (b) that that guilt is capable of being proved. In such an enquiry much will depend upon whether the fault alleged is heretical or moral in character. If the latter the affair will turn very largely upon what can be proved. It is accepted without challenge that drunkenness, embezzlement, gross indecency, are moral faults scandalous in a minister and the only question is whether the accused can be shown to have been guilty of such conduct. If, however, the charge is one of heresy the actual terms of what the minister said or wrote will probably be freely—perhaps proudly—confessed, and the question before the Committee will be as to whether this appears to constitute a heretical opinion of such a character as to demand that the matter be taken further.

Plea by Accused   The Committee may report that in their view no further action need be taken, and if the Presbytery agree then that is the end of the matter. If, on the other hand, the Committee are satisfied there are adequate grounds on which to proceed they should, without elaborating on the matter in any way, simply state this and ask the Presbytery to authorise them to prepare a statement setting forth the heretical opinions or the improper conduct alleged and to submit this to the accused. The accused in due course may plead Guilty in terms of the Statement. Or, again, he may in writing state Objections to the Statement in part or in whole. It is wise that the Presbytery should have given authority to its Special Committee to act for it in the adjusting of the Statement, if that is deemed appropriate in light of the objections received.

Confession   The Act of 1935 says that "if the person concerned shall admit all or any of the allegations contained in the said Statement, the Presbytery shall take such steps as shall seem to it to be necessary and proper according to the nature and extent of the allegations admitted by such person."

In the body of the text of the Sixth Edition (at page 321) Cox states, "If the accused confess, and the matter confessed be of a scandalous nature censurable in others, such as the sin of uncleanness, or some other gross scandal (whatever be the nature of his penitence, though all be convinced of it), the Presbytery is *instanter* to depose him *ab officio.*" This is a reprint of the precise terms of the old Act of 1707. They make it clear that the Presbytery has no discretion in such a situation; it is bound to depose from office. While I should agree that the kind of offence referred to merits the greatest severity I am not myself satisfied that today's Presbytery is bound in this strait-jacket. The Act of 1935 quoted above specifically repeals all prior Acts of Assembly "insofar as any of their provisions are inconsistent with this Act." To me it appears clear that there is a complete inconsistency here and that that being so the later Act must prevail. Besides which, it would seem unjust that deposition should of necessity follow upon confession of guilt whereas proof of guilt after trial leaves it to the Presbytery to depose or to take "such other steps as it shall deem to be necessary and proper".

Deposition The matter is of considerable import-ance because of the utter finality of a sentence of de-position compared with, for example, suspension from office *sine die*. The latter has all the immediate force and effect of the former, but if at some future time the Presbytery is satisfied that the hurt is healed and that the transgressor might be restored to office it has it within its own power to lift the suspension. And this it can do without too much fuss. If the man has been deposed then only the Assembly can restore his status, and this means, of course, an approach to the General Assembly by way of petition which must of necessity rehearse the whole facts and circumstances of the orig-inal offence, giving them anew to the whole Church.

I rather clearly remember a case when a minister who had been deposed at least twenty years earlier petitioned for reinstatement. Interestingly enough, the reason for his having been deprived of status was an irregularity that would not be looked upon half so seriously today as it had been at the time. The principal effect of bringing the whole affair to light was one of widespread dismay that so serious a consequence should have followed on so slight an offence, and the crave of the petition was granted without demur. That is the only case that has occurred within my recollection, and I am prepared to believe that the reason is that others, though they might well deserve to be reinstated, would rather leave things as they are than have the unhappy episode dragged out into the glare of the television lights on the Assembly floor.

Preparation of Libel The document setting forth the charge is known in ecclesiastical parlance as a "libel" and the whole process is referred to as "trial by libel". Assuming that the accused has wholly, or at least substantially, denied the conduct attributed to him in the Statement, a libel is to be prepared and subscribed by the Moderator and Clerk of Presbytery. Before being served it is to be reviewed by the Procurator of the Church. The accused person at the time when the libel is served upon him should also be furnished with a list of the witnesses to be called by the Presbytery.

Committee to Conduct Trial A Presbytery is a most unwieldy body to conduct a trial, particularly if it is going to involve examining many witnesses and is likely to occupy a fair amount of time. Provision therefore exists whereby the Presbytery may appoint a Committee of not less than three and not more than five of its number to act for it. It may also ask that two members be appointed from the Board of Assessors (a panel of knowledgeable persons appointed by the General Assembly) to sit with the others as "the court for the trial of the cause". The Presbytery shall also appoint one of its number (two if it so determine) to act as prosecutor, and he in turn may instruct counsel or engage a solicitor to act in the affair. The Presbytery may well feel constrained to engage—and pay— someone to represent the accused.

Suspension At this point the Presbytery may, depending upon the whole circumstances, resolve that the accused should be suspended from the exercise of his ministerial functions until the case has been disposed of, and if so it shall make an order accordingly and appoint an interim moderator to act with the Kirk Session. The minister's right to his stipend shall, however, be in no way affected by such suspension.

Special Defence Within twenty-one days of receipt of the libel the accused may lodge Notice of a Special Defence—that he was in quite another place when the offence occurred (alibi) or that he was mentally deranged at the time. Since resort to a special defence transfers the *onus probandi* to the shoulders of the defender he ought when lodging his Special Defence to provide a list of the witnesses he proposes to call in support of it.

Opening Sederunt of Trial Once this has all been done a date shall be fixed for the trial to begin, and not less than seven days' notice thereof shall be given to the accused. At this first sitting the accused shall have the opportunity of stating any objection to the competency of the proceedings, to the constitution of the court, to the relevancy of the libel, or indeed to make any other preliminary objection he may have to the regularity of the proceedings. As was hinted earlier, if the charge is one of heresy the whole burden of the case may turn on an objection to relevance—that the facts alleged do not disclose any deviation from orthodoxy. Once that question has been settled one way or the other the case is ended.

Diet of Proof Assuming that these various matters have been disposed of and the facts are still open to challenge, the Committee shall appoint a date when the cause is to go to proof. At the said diet all evidence shall be given on oath—first witnesses for the prosecution then those for the defence, with cross-examination and re-examination. A shorthand writer shall have been employed and put on oath and a record of the evidence shall be taken. Speeches shall be made for the prosecution and then for the defence. If it is the Presbytery itself which has heard the evidence it shall then go on to issue its verdict. If the hearing has been remitted to a Committee that body shall prepare a report of its findings in fact. If it is a unanimous report then the Presbytery shall be bound to accept its conclusions and find accordingly. If the report is that of a majority the Presbytery may resolve either to accept the verdict or to have the evidence printed and of new to hear the parties (not the witnesses). It shall then reach its verdict.

Incidentally, the verdict shall be one either of Proven or of Not Proven—not of Guilty or Not Guilty. This is sometimes made the subject of criticism on the ground that a verdict of Not Proven leaves a stain on a man's character. Some would go so far as to interpret it as meaning "he did it but they couldn't pin it on him". For myself I have always taken the view that the Church is right in its choice of this verdict and that it is the courts of the land that are wrong. A man accused of something pleads Guilty or Not Guilty. If the latter the case goes to trial when either the accusation is proved or it is not proved. The question of the man's innocence is strictly irrelevant. I remember a very famous case in the High Court where a boy was convicted of murder. The fact was proved beyond a peradventure, but on appeal it was held that the police had resorted to unfair means in their early examination of the boy, judgment

102 A GUIDE TO THE PRESBYTERY

was recalled, and he was set free. Did that mean he was Not Guilty? Surely not. It did mean that according to the rules governing such matters the accusation had not been proved. But, if I may mix my metaphors, do not let me get side-tracked on to a hobby-horse.

Sentence By whichever of the above methods the verdict has been reached, if it be a verdict of Proven (Guilty) the Presbytery shall hear the offender or his representative in mitigation. It shall then go on to consider what is the appropriate censure and "direct what steps shall be taken for carrying the censure into effect". The censures of the Church are admonition, rebuke, suspension from office (either for a period or *sine die*), deposition, or, in cases of extreme aggravation and contumacy, excommunication. If a minister be suspended or deposed he is debarred from performing any of the functions of the ministry including the conduct of public worship. Admonition and rebuke are administered by the Moderator in face of the court. Suspension from office debars from the privileges as well as the duties of the ministry. Where it is for a limited period and involves a minister living in a manse special arrangements will have to be come to in this regard.

Record Apart It is provided that the whole record of the proceedings in a libel case are to be kept in a Record Apart. If the proceedings end with a finding of guilt and a pronouncing of censure then there shall be entered in the ordinary minute-book of the Presbytery the first minute of the Record Apart, the terms of the libel, and the verdict and sentence. If the case ends in complete acquittal then the Record Apart and all papers in the case shall be sealed and held *in retentis* for five years, after which they shall be destroyed.

Proceedings in Other Courts The proceedings and judgments of other courts, civil or criminal, cannot be accepted as a substitute for independent action in the courts of the Church. For example, citation as co-defender in an undefended divorce action does not prove adultery, nor does conviction on a charge of driving with an excess of alcohol in the blood prove drunkenness. Though a plea of Guilty tendered by the minister before the Sheriff in the latter case would be a very significant item of evidence.

A difficulty can arise when a criminal charge is being preferred at the instance of the police in that they have the first claim on all the productions, and in any case are likely to have been first on the scene and impounded them. Let it be that a minister is being charged with embezzlement—the police will certainly have taken possession of all books, vouchers, etc. and, until there has been a criminal trial or the fiscal has decided not to proceed to trial, these papers will not be available for the Presbytery's prosecutor. In their absence there is clearly nothing he can do to establish a case. Police and fiscal are likely to prove co-operative, but the situation is a difficult one and I cannot suggest a solution.

Demission on Grounds of Ill-Health It is not unknown in a case where a minister has become involved in some censurable activity for him to offer to demit his charge on the strength of a medical certificate. And it is not unknown for the Presbytery to see in this a nice tidy way out of a messy situation. The congregation concerned, since he is resigning as their minister, are not likely to make difficulties. For the Presbytery to avail itself of this way of escape is made all the easier by the fact that there is provision whereby when a

minister demits his charge the Presbyterial Certificate
to which he would normally have been entitled may at
the sole discretion of the Presbytery be withheld—the
phrase used is "unless the Presbytery, for due cause
shown, resolve to withhold the same." In the
circumstances outlined it is unlikely that the defaulting
minister is going to demand a certificate since this is
in effect to force the hand of the Presbytery into
proceeding by way of trial by libel. In any case, a
minister whose certificate has been thus withheld is
entitled at the expiry of two years to ask for its
restoration.

This is far from being a wholly satisfactory solution.
It might be said to amount to the accused agreeing to
two years' suspension in lieu of trial. If the grounds of
health averred on the medical certificate are such as to
take away any semblance of moral fault or delinquency
then it seems unfair to refuse to declare that the man's
character and conduct are becoming his profession and
give him a certificate to this effect. If, on the other
hand, the minister's conduct has been such as to justify
withholding (without trial) the certificate then the
matter should in justice have been taken further. When
at the end of two years the delinquent comes to the
Presbytery to ask for the restoration of the certificate
there can be no obligation upon him to "prove his
innocence"—the obligation still lies squarely with the
Presbytery either to grant his request or to prove his
guilt. After the passage of all that time this could prove
a difficult, if not actually an impossible, task as well as
being a most distasteful exercise.

It appears to me that a Presbytery faced with the
situation of a *fama* will be well advised to consider most
carefully what is the wise and just course for it to

pursue. It is all too easy to identify Christian charity with the search for a painless way out of a difficult and unpleasant situation.

Loss of Status   Care has to be taken of the distinction between loss of office and loss of status. In the case of a minister, of course, the latter will always include the former. Suspension from office will, while it runs, debar a minister from performing any ministerial function just as effectively as if he had been deprived of his status.

Students of Theology

Presbyteries have from time to time been reminded by the General Assembly that they have a responsibility for seeking to promote recruitment to the ministry. While the numbers coming forward today are adequate to maintain manpower it is an unhappy feature of the contemporary picture that, comparatively speaking, so small a proportion is being drawn from the rural areas or from the Highlands and Islands. And while it is good that we should be recruiting many "mature students" it is regrettable that not more are coming straight into training for the ministry—I hesitate to call them "immature students"!

Selection School   It must be apparent that success in the ministry demands more than mere academic ability. There are those who for reasons of personality make-up are just not suited for the task. No amount of sense of vocation, no degree of dedication to the work, can compensate for basic unsuitability. Hence the introduction some years ago of the idea of the Selection

School. Anyone today hoping to enter upon a course of study for the ministry is required to make application to the Assembly's Committee on Education for the Ministry which will arrange for him to attend a Selection School. This is a short residential course at which the aspirant is submitted to the most intense scrutiny by a carefully selected panel of examiners with a view to assessing his suitability to discharge the varied duties of the ministry. An applicant unsuccessful on the first occasion may apply again at a later time—up to a maximum of three trials in all. The Committee is to inform the Presbytery concerned of the results of appearances at the School, and the Presbytery is to bear in mind in a pastoral context the serious implications which a negative decision could have on a candidate with a deep sense of vocation.

An inevitable weakness is that a candidate can enrol for classes in divinity although not accepted by the Church of Scotland as a candidate for its ministry and, if turned down at Selection School, is quite likely to do this while awaiting a second attempt. The process continues till the final refusal, by which time the course may be largely—and successfully—completed. A desperately unhappy situation can emerge.

Nomination by Presbytery The business of actually nominating candidates for the ministry of the Church is still the affair of the Presbytery, and applications for such nomination are to be made at any time after application for acceptance has been lodged with the Assembly's Committee. Such application may be made after acceptance by the Committee, but must be before the beginning of the course of theological study. The Presbytery has to satisfy itself that the applicant is a member of the Church of Scotland, has been accepted by the Assembly's Committee, and is, in character, conduct, and belief a suitable person for the office of the ministry. Nomination should be made by Presbytery not later than 17th September in the year in which the candidate wishes to begin his studies.

Supervision by Presbytery Every recognised student for the ministry will remain under the supervision of the Presbytery which nominated him except in the case where he has been regularly transferred to the care of another Presbytery. Such transfer is effected by securing and lodging a certificate of character. In all matters affecting his candidature the decision of the supervising Presbytery shall be final, with a right to the candidate to petition the General Assembly for review of the Presbytery's decision. This would seem to relieve the Presbytery of the obligation to have the candidate at its bar when the hostile decision is reached.

Discipline Though it is difficult to find authority for this, I should certainly take the view that if a Divinity Student is guilty of some grave moral lapse it is for the Assembly's Committee in consultation with the Presbytery to consider his position in relation to the continuance or otherwise of his candidature. The actual exercise of discipline, however, I should take to be the affair of the Kirk Session of the congregation to which he belongs.

Trials for Licence Not later than 30th November in his final year each student is to apply to the Presbytery having supervision over him to be taken on trials for licence. Before doing this he has to intimate to the Assembly's Committee his intention so to apply. Early in November a complete list of these anticipated applications is sent to the Clerks of all the Presbyteries of the Church with an indication that the Presbytery may take exception to any of the candidates.

"The object of trials for licence shall be to enable the Presbytery to ensure that an applicant for licence is acquainted with the present legal and sacramental practice and past tradition of the Church of Scotland, and that he is a fit person to proceed to the ministry." The trials are in two parts—a *viva voce* examination in the principles and practice of the Kirk, and the conduct of a principal service of public worship in the presence of a minister and elder appointed by the Presbytery.

Exit Certificate When the full course has been completed to the satisfaction of the College authorities and of the Assembly's Committee, an Exit Certificate is sent to the Clerk of the supervising Presbytery which, if it has sustained the trials, may then proceed to the Service of Licensing. This will normally be held on the evening of a weeknight in a suitable Church within the bounds, though if there is only one candidate the service may appropriately be held in the Church of which he is a member. It is usual for each licentiate to be presented with a copy of the Scriptures which he is being authorised to "open" to the people.

Our fathers in their day were very clear as to the impropriety of preaching being undertaken by any who had not reached the stage of licence. Writing some ninety years ago Mair has some pithy observations on the subject of students in pulpits. "Ministers," he writes, "are expressly prohibited from giving countenance or permission to students to engage in the public ministry of the Word before being regularly licensed to preach the Gospel. Hitherto the Church has considered that on the one hand the conducting of public worship was a service not to be grasped at, or even undertaken, immaturely, and that on the other hand the time and powers of students were required for, and ought to be devoted to, their own studies. It is remarkable that in these days, when the field of study is so much enlarged, and the need of it so much greater, there should appear some inclination to permit, and even to encourage, students to leave their proper work and hasten to the pulpit."

Changed days, changed ways!

Probationers

The terms "probationer" and "licentiate" have over the years been used indiscriminately of those who, having completed satisfactorily their course in the Faculty of Divinity, have been licensed by the Presbytery as Preachers of the Gospel. Of recent years, however, there has been an attempt to draw a distinction, using the term "probationer" to design those who, having been licensed, are serving or have completed the probationary period required of those who intend to go forward to a charge and pursue the work of the regular ministry, and reserving the term "licentiate" for those who, having achieved the status which licence confers (as Preachers of the Gospel), are content to leave the matter there and seek their living in some other occupation. Time was when those in the former class were referred to (for obvious reasons) as "expectants", but that term has disappeared from the contemporary vocabulary.

Period of Probation A student for the ministry on being licensed by his Presbytery is to be given an Extract of Licence—and this he should retain as proof of his status. Unless in the most exceptional circumstances, every Probationer is required to serve,

for the period until the end of the April following
licence, in an assistantship to which he is directed by
the Assembly's Committee on Education for the
Ministry. If this "probationary year" is not sustained
he may be required to serve a further year, probably
in a different assistantship. During his period of
probationary service he is under the conjoint supervision of the Assembly's Committee and of the Presbytery, but when his probation has been satisfactorily
completed and he has been given a certificate to this
effect the situation is reported to the Assembly's Committee on Probationers and Transference and Admission of Ministers who have a responsibility for him
in his search for a parish, but he comes under the sole
supervision of the Presbytery. In the event of his
moving to a new district he should obtain from his
Clerk of Presbytery a certificate as to character and
conduct and should lodge this within two months,
along with sight of his Extract of Licence, with the
Clerk of the Presbytery within whose bounds he has
come to reside or to work.

Admitted by General Assembly   It happens occasionally that a Probationer from another denomination is
accepted by the General Assembly with that status,
and it sometimes happens, too, that a minister of
another denomination is accepted but with the status
of a Probationer. It is usual in the latter case that some
further education (certain specified classes to be
attended at College) or further training (probably an
assistantship in a parish) is required, and it is
invariable custom that the person concerned is put
under the supervision of a particular Presbytery. It is, I
think, universally accepted that there is no need to take
such a person on trials with a view to licence, but that

he has been received with the full status of a
Probationer so that once he has fulfilled the conditions
imposed by the Assembly he is free to accept a Call to a
parish. It may seem odd, though, that we should be
prepared to assume in the case of these "outsiders"
that degree of "acquaintance with the present legal
and sacramental practice and past tradition of the
Church of Scotland" on which we are so careful to
examine those who have grown up in that tradition. A
Probationer received in this way stands in identically
the same relationship to the Presbytery as does a
person who has been licensed by it in the normal way.

Ordination   A Presbytery has power to agree to the
ordination of a Probationer in circumstances other
than his appointment to a charge. If the Probationer
has been appointed to a posting abroad by the
Overseas Council there may be a request for him to be
ordained before he departs, although it should be
added that increasingly today ordination is given at the
hands of the indigenous Church within which he is to
serve. Commissioning as a Chaplain to the Forces, or
appointment to a full-time Hospital, Industrial, or
University chaplaincy, or to a Community Ministry
will always involve ordination, and this in the case
of the Missionary or Forces Chaplain will be sought
from the Presbytery under whose jurisdiction the
Probationer presently is, or, in the other cases, from
that within whose bounds is situated the post which he
is about to fill.

It is not uncommon that the ordination of an
Assistant is asked for by the Minister and Kirk Session
of the charge within which he is serving. It is
recommended in an Assembly deliverance that before
sympathetic consideration is given to such a request

the Probationer should have been acting in the parish for a period of at least six months, and that he should give an undertaking to continue there for at least a further eighteen months after ordination. The Service of Ordination will be held in the Church in which he is serving unless there is some compelling reason why it should be held elsewhere.

A Presbytery is not bound to accede to a request for ordination. The General Assembly of 1969 laid down two general rules in this context—that ordination should be conferred only (1) where the Church has some control over, and right to approve of, the appointment, and a continuing general oversight of how the "charge" is being worked; and (2) where there is substantial and real need for the person regularly to baptise or to celebrate Communion. The Assembly of 1982 refused the petition for ordination submitted by a Licentiate acting as a teacher of religious education in school.

In all the cases referred to above, although the ordination does not involve induction to a parish, an edict in common form should be served on two Sundays, and this will be appropriately done either in the Church where the ordination is to take place or in that of which the ordinand is a member.

Discipline In all matters of life and doctrine the Probationer or Licentiate is subject to the Presbytery —notwithstanding the responsibility laid upon the Assembly's Committee for the oversight of his work during the probationary period. Should some *fama* arise concerning a Probationer the Presbytery has to proceed exactly as in the case of a Minister.

Lay Missionaries

The Lay Missionary is an agent of the Home Department of the General Assembly. His candidature must be approved by the Presbytery within whose bounds he normally resides at the time of application, that body being satisfied of his strong Christian character and that he is a member of the Church of Scotland. After a year's probation he may, at the instigation of the Home Department, be commissioned "by the General Assembly or such subordinate court as may be named by the General Assembly". This, I imagine, is almost certain to be a Presbytery, though I suppose it could be a Synod—I have never known it to be the General Assembly itself, and I cannot believe it could be a Kirk Session. When the commissioning is in the hands of a Presbytery it involves an *in hunc effectum* meeting and a service in the Church where the missionary is serving or is about to serve. Presbyteries are informed by the Home Department when Lay Missionaries under their care have been transferred from one sphere of service to another, but it is for the missionary himself to secure from the Presbytery which he is leaving a certificate as to life and character and to lodge this immediately with the Clerk of the Presbytery to which he has gone.

The Lay Missionary preaches and exercises pastoral care under the direction of a Minister and Kirk Session. Although the Regulations do not say so (Regulation 2, 1961) it is my opinion that in the matter of the discharge of his duties the Lay Missionary is answerable to the Home Department which employs him while in the matter of life and doctrine he is answerable in the first instance to his Kirk Session.

There is now provision whereby the Lay Missionary is, in virtue of his office, a Corresponding Member of Presbytery (see page 13). That apart, however, he may be, and generally is, admitted as an elder in the congregation in which he serves, and in that capacity, of course, he may be elected Representative Elder to the Presbytery or chosen by the Presbytery itself as an Additional Elder. This does not affect in any way his answerability to the Kirk Session.

The Diaconate

"A Deacon or Deaconess is one who has, under a Call from God, pledged himself or herself to the service of Jesus Christ and His Church, and has been trained and commissioned thereto in conformity with the doctrine of the Church of Scotland." (Since at the time of writing all members of the Diaconate are in fact Deaconesses I propose to speak of "she" throughout, though this should be read as "he or she".) A Deaconess may be licensed to preach the Word, and regular preaching and conduct of worship shall be confined to those so licensed. The rules governing the licensing of Deaconesses as Preachers were introduced in a day before the regular ministry was open to women. The course of study is in effect that for the ordained ministry. It is difficult to believe that many (if any) would take this course with a view to entering the diaconate rather than the ministry. It is difficult, too, to understand why in today's climate the full right of entry into pulpits should be confined to a small group within the diaconate. One might look for some changes in these regards in the near future.

Preparation   Application for acceptance in training has to be made to the Diaconate Board. It is required of the Deaconess that she be a communicant member of the Church of Scotland and over 21 years of age, that she have undergone the appropriate training and have been commissioned by a Presbytery, and, when licence to preach is involved, that she have been so licensed by a Presbytery. The choice of candidates is made by the Diaconate Board, which notifies the Presbytery for its interest, but when licence to preach is involved the Diaconate Board has also to commend the candidate to the appropriate Presbytery for nomination as a theological student. In all cases the Diaconate Board prescribes a probationary period, which it may extend if it deems this wise, and it has to inform the Presbytery within whose bounds the probationary period is being served.

It is for the Presbytery to arrange and conduct a Service of Commissioning. When the candidate is also to be licensed this too will be in the hands of the Presbytery and will normally be undertaken at the same service as the commissioning. There is no question of taking the candidate on trials for such licensing.

As is the case with a Lay Missionary the Deaconess now sits as a Corresponding Member of Presbytery, and, if an elder and member of Kirk Session, she may be appointed Representative Elder by that Kirk Session or Additional Elder by the Presbytery itself.

Answerability   For the due performance of her services a Deaconess is declared to be answerable (a) when she is serving with a Department or Committee of the Church to that Department or Committee, or (b) when she is in the employment of a secular organisation to that organisation. That is to say, a Deaconess working in a parish is answerable not to the Minister or Kirk Session but to the Home Department which employs her. For the day to day ordering of affairs, of course, she takes instruction from the Minister.

In matters of life and doctrine the Deaconess is answerable to the Presbytery within whose bounds she is serving, or if not serving within the bounds of a Presbytery to that which commissioned her.

On moving from the bounds of one Presbytery to those of another a Deaconess is required to present a Presbyterial Certificate as to character and conduct. Presbyteries are to maintain Rolls of Deaconesses in active service, on probation, in training, or retired as the case may be, within their bounds and are to include in the first list the names of those whom they have commissioned and who are now serving furth of Scotland.

Readers

Readers are members of the Church, men or women, who, having received special training, have been invested with authority to conduct worship anywhere in the Church.

The Office　The Office of Reader is one of very ancient origin. The new Church of the Reformation that emerged in Scotland in the latter half of the sixteenth century was inevitably acutely short of qualified ministers — and they placed great stress upon the "qualified". It is true that those priests who had embraced the principles of the Reformation — and there seem to have been many of them—were restored to their former livings, but only after due training. And this, naturally, took time. In the interval many parishes were served by Readers under the general direction and control of Superintendents—a system not unlike the Methodist circuit principle of today. The supply of ministers steadily increased and as the parishes began to be filled the Office of Reader was allowed to lapse. It was, however, officially revived at the end of the First World War, again with a view to relieving a critical emergency situation. Again the office fell into desuetude until it was once more revived in 1958. The present situation is governed by an Act of 1974.

Candidature A person wishing to become a Reader must, in the first place, submit to the Presbytery of his residence or of his congregation an application accompanied by a letter from his minister as to character and experience in Church work, and by an extract minute of Kirk Session supporting his application. The Presbytery, having satisfied itself as to the candidate's suitability, refers the matter to the Assembly's Department of Education which arranges a suitable course of study to be undertaken under the care of a minister as tutor. When the prescribed course has been satisfactorily completed the Presbytery will arrange to have the candidate admitted to the Office of Reader, which will be after he has answered a series of questions and signed the Formula. The setting apart may be done at a Presbytery meeting or at a service specially appointed for the purpose.

Supervision Supervision of Readers is to be exercised by Presbyteries and should include an annual appearance of the Readers before the court. A certificate of character and status should be obtained by a Reader leaving the bounds of a Presbytery and should immediately on arrival in a new area be lodged with the Clerk of that Presbytery. Once every two years Readers are expected to attend an in-service conference arranged by the Department of Education. Each Presbytery maintains a List of the Readers within its bounds, and the complete list is printed annually in the Year Book. At his own request a Reader may have his name taken from the "active list" without affecting his status as a Reader.

So far as life and doctrine are concerned a Reader must, in my view, be subject to the Kirk Session of the congregation to which he belongs, although in the event of its being alleged, for example, that he was preaching heretical opinions it would be for the Presbytery to conduct an enquiry even if in the end they passed the matter to the Kirk Session for further process and censure. Meantime, I think, the Presbytery could order the removal of the offender's name from its List.

Availability The unfortunate feature of this institution is that Readers are in most plentiful supply where the demand for their services is at its lowest, and that they are thin on the ground where they could most profitably be employed. In the areas of conurbation Readers are heard complaining (with justice) that they have equipped themselves to do a job and are anxious to get on with it but that only very rarely are their services called upon. In some of the more remote districts, on the other hand, ministers may be heard complaining (with equal justice) that they cannot get a Sunday off duty because of the expense of bringing supply from some far-off city and that there are no

Readers, or not nearly enough Readers, available in their area. While accepting both of these criticisms as justified it is difficult to see where the answer lies.

Auxiliary Ministry

The Auxiliary Ministry is an institution of very recent creation—indeed at the time of writing there are no auxiliary ministers within the service of the Church although there are a few in training.

Origin The idea of creating such a ministry originated with the Committee of Forty. Two principles seem to have been in mind. First, that something should be devised to enable the Kirk to avail itself of what many believe to be a great untapped pool of service within the ordinary membership—though it may seem odd if the way to avail ourselves of the service of the layman begins by ordaining him so that he no longer is a layman. Secondly, that steps should be taken to deal with two difficult situations—first, the case where you have an isolated community which requires to be ministered to but could never qualify for, much less maintain, a full-scale traditional ministry; and, secondly, the case where you have an overworked city minister desperately in need of assistance which is just not available and for which in any case his congregation could not afford to pay. Accordingly an Act was passed in 1980 and, as I have indicated, men are now in training in terms of its provisions.

Definition "An Auxiliary Minister is a person who has been ordained for life to a ministry of Word and Sacrament exercisable under supervision on a part-time and non-stipendiary basis." The Act makes it

abundantly clear that no-one in virtue of being an
Auxiliary Minister is to be eligible for induction to a
charge. Our long-held and deeply-cherished principle
of the parity of the ministry—a tradition which I
believe to be based upon sound Presbyterian
principles—has been discarded in favour of a two-tier
system. For, let us be under no illusions, a ministry
which is part-time, part-trained, unpaid, and debarred
from induction to a charge cannot escape a second-
class status—even if it wanted to do so.

Candidature   Recruitment of candidates is to be "in
the first instance a function of Presbyteries", and in
discharging this function they are "to have regard to
the existing and anticipated demands of the charges
within their bounds." This appears to mean that a
Presbytery is to have the assignment in view before it
looks for the candidate, though it is difficult to
reconcile this with the fact that the course is one of two
years' duration followed by a year of probation—the
"existing demands" could have altered not a little in
three years.

The aspirant is to make formal application to the
Assembly's Committee on Education for the Ministry
to be accepted as a candidate. He must be a member of
the Church of Scotland and must produce recommendations from his minister, his Kirk Session, and
his Presbytery. If the Committee is satisfied with the
appellant's credentials it shall inform the Presbytery
accordingly and the latter body shall formally nominate him for the course.

Course of Training   The Committee on Education for
the Ministry is to regulate the course of training, and
this may vary according to the academic qualifications
and general background of the candidate. The course

shall be part-time and shall involve participation in central and residential training and extension study under supervision both of a local and of a central tutor. It shall last for twenty-four months. In each academic year the candidate shall be attached for six months in a parish, and this shall not normally be his home parish. It is the Presbytery which is to satisfy itself in each of the two years of study as to the candidate's continuing progress and suitability and it is to submit a report thereon to the Assembly's Committee which shall have the responsibility of sustaining the course, and if it does so it is to issue an Exit Certificate. The Act does not say how the Presbytery is to secure evidence on which to reach a judgment on the candidate's academic progress.

Licence At the end of the course the Presbytery is to take the candidate on trials for licence—that is to say, in respect of his preaching and conduct of worship, and of his knowledge of Church law and of the Sacraments—and if satisfied is to proceed "to license him to the Auxiliary Ministry of the Church of Scotland." It would appear to be intended that these trials should be identical with those for the regular ministry. It is significant, though, that the candidate for the regular ministry is licensed "to preach the Gospel of the Lord Jesus Christ and to exercise his gifts as a Probationer for the Holy Ministry", whereas in this other case the candidate is being "licensed to the Auxiliary Ministry of the Church of Scotland". There is here a distinction which I cannot believe is intended to mark a difference.

Ordination In all ordinary cases a year's probation is to be served after licence. It would appear (though it is not stated) that it is for the Education for the

Ministry Committee to arrange such probationary service, and it is certainly for that Committee to receive a report from the supervising minister and to declare whether it is satisfied therewith. Ordination is to be by Presbytery and, though it is not clear, it would seem that contrary to long-established custom ordination is not to be restricted to the case where the licentiate has already been assigned to an appointment. In exceptional circumstances the probationary year may be waived, and in that case "ordination may follow immediately upon the satisfactory completion of the course." If, as the Regulations appended to the Act clearly state, "ordination is to follow immediately upon the satisfactory completion of the course" then licence has been by-passed in this instance and this particular class of candidate has been freed both of the need to serve a probationary year and also of the need to undergo trials for licence. This seems odd. Further, the provision seems clearly to confirm my observation above about ordination being, as it were, in a vacuum —that is, not dependent upon an assignment having been awarded.

Assignment "Auxiliary Ministers may be allotted to such assignments as the Presbytery of the bounds may from time to time determine." The conditions governing the assignment (including the minimum amount of time to be devoted to it by the Auxiliary and the arrangements for the payment of pulpit supply fees and for the reimbursement of expenses) are to be defined by the Presbytery in writing after consultation with the minister or interim moderator and Kirk Session of the parish within which the Auxiliary is to operate. "Initially the duration of each assignment should not exceed five years." This seems clearly to imply that every assignment is to be for a specific period set forth in writing. But "the Presbytery shall be entitled at any time ... to suspend or terminate the assignment", to renew it for up to another five years, or to vary its terms. The assignment with its terms in writing has all the appearance of a contract of service and it is difficult to believe these terms can be altered, much less that the assignment itself can be terminated, on the say-so of one side alone. For myself I feel that the Auxiliary must at least have a right of appeal against an arbitrary termination of an assignment which he had undertaken for a specific period. Since there is no remuneration, termination does not involve a financial loss, but it is still something which the Auxiliary may justly resent and against which he should have a remedy.

Nothing is said about how far the Auxiliary is bound by the terms of the assignment. Must he complete the five years? If not, what kind of notice is he to give? Or what if he should want to be moved to another assignment? The Regulations raise more questions than they supply answers.

Throughout the duration of the assignment the Auxiliary is to be a member of the Presbytery of the bounds, and to be associated with the Kirk Session of the parish within which he is working. He may act as Moderator *pro tempore* of the Kirk Session, strictly on the conditions that apply to such moderators—that is, for the conduct only of specific items of business listed by the regular moderator. All of this shall terminate immediately the assignment ends.

Nothing at all is said as to whether there is to be some form of service to mark the beginning of an assignment. The initial assignment might be marked by holding the service of ordination (if he has not already been ordained) in the Church where he is to be working. But what of subsequent assignments? Obviously there cannot be any kind of induction, but some overt act might seem to be called for.

Answerability   For the conduct of the duties of his assignment the Auxiliary Minister is to be "subject to the oversight and supervision of a minister or ministers appointed by the Presbytery of the bounds." I imagine this would have to be the minister or interim moderator of the parish in which the Auxiliary is working, for if it were any other minister we should be coming dangerously near to a situation of "intrusion". It is also to be presumed, I think, that the Auxiliary Minister should have some right of appeal to the Presbytery in the event of difficulty or disagreement arising in this field.

Although the matter is not dealt with in the Act it is, I think, to be presumed that as an ordained minister the Auxiliary shall, in respect of life and doctrine, come under the discipline of the Presbytery. I take it too that his ordination will be preceded by the serving of an edict in common form and that this will be done in the Church of which he is a member.

It is also, I imagine, to be presumed that while a ministerial member of Presbytery the Auxiliary will be eligible to be returned at any time as a commissioner to the General Assembly, and that while he is not actively involved in an assignment and therefore does not have a seat in Presbytery he may be invited to attend Presbytery as a Corresponding Member.

Difficulties   From all that I have said in the foregoing attempt to expiscate the Act it must be apparent that I am not at all happy with it. I have not set out deliberately to be critical, but it is difficult to explain clearly something which is basically confused, as I believe to be the case here. It is never a good sign of any legislation when too much is left to be presumed. Doubtless many of the points will be clarified as time passes and experience is gained.

No matter how much this may be true, however, there is, it seems to me, one very serious problem that is bound to cause trouble, and to do so sooner rather than later. This has to do with the non-stipendiary aspect of this type of ministry. To visualise an auxiliary ministry as a wholly voluntary contribution to the work of the Kirk by someone who has another job and another means of livelihood sounds very ideal. To me, though, it seems unrealistic to imagine that men (or women) are going to submit themselves to this degree of training, to bind themselves to a minimum number of hours per week of the most demanding work, and to put themselves under the direction and control of others in the performance of it, if there is to be no financial return beyond the recovery of their outlays. Further, it would seem that if an Auxiliary's assignment involves preaching he is to receive the pulpit supply fees, whereas if his work is exclusively of a pastoral character he is to be completely without remuneration. It seems to me there are here the seeds of trouble and discontent. And then what about the congregations enjoying the services of the Auxiliaries? I can imagine some resentment on the part of Congregation A which has to find a stipend while Congregation B further up the glen enjoys the services of a non-stipendiary. Or of Congregation C which is hard put to it to meet the not inconsiderable expense of employing a Probationer in his year of compulsory service while Congregation D across the way has a non-stipendiary for the cost of his bus fares.

Apropos of the point about pulpit supply I must add that I am assured by the Secretaries of the Church and Ministry Department that it is understood that pulpit supply fees will not be paid to the Auxiliary in respect of any preaching he may do in the pulpit of the charge to which he has been assigned, but that he will be free to accept payment for supply given in any other charge. I have been quite unable to find support for this contention within the Act itself. Section 11 of the Act says that the terms of any assignment are to "include provisions regarding payment of supply fees". Admittedly it says further that this is "subject to Section 1". And Section 1 speaks of the non-stipendiary basis of the Auxiliary Ministry. All that Section 1 does, however, is to mention the word "non-stipendiary" and it does nothing to define it. I find it hard to believe that a pulpit supply fee can be regarded as a "stipend", and I fail to understand what "provision" has to be made "regarding the payment of supply fees" if in fact they are not to be paid at all. If what is meant in Section 11 is that pulpit supply fees are not to be paid to the Auxiliary then it would be hard indeed to discover a more devious or misleading way of saying so. And if that is what the position is to be it adds a further anomaly to those already listed—that the Auxiliary who is non-fee-receiving in his assignment is not so when he goes from home.

There seems considerable urgency for the whole affair to be reviewed and an Act framed which is clear and tight. Presbyteries are to have the responsibility of operating the scheme—they are entitled to something much less ambiguous than the present Act.

6

What It Works At

REVIEWING JUDGMENTS

In all that has been written so far about the business of the Presbytery we have been viewing it as a court of first instance, that is to say, as the court which either initiates the business at its own hand, or which, by statute or by practice, is the court in which the issue is first heard. The Presbytery, however, has a quite separate and distinctive function in that, standing as it does between the Kirk Session and the Synod in our hierarchy of courts, it has to act as a court of appeal in almost every matter in which a Kirk Session has jurisdiction, as well as having power to review decisions of congregational meetings and, in a limited way, of Deacons' Courts, of Congregational Boards, and even, I should contend, of Committees of Management.

Machinery of Review

It may be appropriate at this stage to set forth in some detail an account of the way in which the courts of the Church handle the business of review. If you are not satisfied with the judgment of a Church court how do you go about having it set aside? In general terms it may be said that there are four ways in which a matter resolved in one court may be brought under review of a superior court—(a) appeal, (b) dissent and complaint, (c) petition, and (d) reference. Let us take them one at a time—though, for reasons which I hope to explain, the first two must be taken as a pair. And to avoid needless complication let's look at them at this stage exclusively as if what was desired was to bring a decision of Presbytery under review of Synod. The procedure is essentially the same no matter from what court you are setting out upon your upward journey.

Appeal : Dissent and Complaint

The procedure in these two cases is identical, but there is an important distinction between them and the use of the wrong nomenclature has in the past proved fatal. The distinction is really a peculiarly simple one. If the party at the bar is dissatisfied with the judgment of the Presbytery he appeals, if a member of the Presbytery is at variance with the judgment of his court he dissents and complains. Why the distinction sometimes appears a little complicated is, I think, partly due to the fact that if, in the latter case quoted above, the disgruntled member of Presbytery having gone to the Synod by dissent and complaint is there defeated and still wants to pursue the matter he has to go to the Assembly—this time by appeal. This, of course, because he was at the bar of the Synod, and from the bar your remedy is appeal. The matter is really supremely straightforward if it is remembered that the party at the bar says, "I appeal", while the member on the bench says, "I dissent and complain".

In what follows in this section I propose to speak simply of appeal, it being understood that everything said applies in identically the same way in the case of dissent and complaint.

When to Appeal An appeal has to be taken at the time when the judgment is arrived at, though there is a single exception to this rule (page 140). In most courts you get at least a few days in which to lodge an appeal, but not so in the courts of the Church. The Standing Orders of the Presbytery of Glasgow allow an appeal to be taken at any time during the course of the sederunt at which the judgment was pronounced. The reason for making this provision was a belief that in the excitement of the moment of hearing the judgment a party may easily miss out on intimating his desire to appeal, and it would seem unfair if on that account he was for ever debarred from taking the matter further. The wise course, clearly, is to appeal the finding as soon as you have heard it's against you, purely as a matter of course and with a view to keeping your options open, and then at your leisure to decide whether or not you wish to pursue it. But not all "parties" are all that completely on the ball.

Normally the party or parties, having presented their case and answered questions, will have been removed from the bar to allow the court to debate the issue. When a decision has been reached parties will be recalled to the bar and the Moderator will formally intimate the judgment to them. At that point the party, if he wishes to take the matter further, ought properly to say, "I protest for leave to appeal", although so long as he makes his intention clear I cannot believe any Presbytery would make an issue regarding the actual phraseology used. The party in fact often in my experience "begs leave to appeal", but this, while it may sound properly respectful, is misleading in that the right to appeal is there to his hand and the Presbytery can do nothing to withhold it—he doesn't need to "beg" for it. Indeed a Presbytery is acting very

dangerously if it tries in any way to prevent or obstruct
him in pursuing his appeal. I have heard the attempt
made to discourage the party by telling him it would
not be competent for the Synod to deal with this on
appeal. Although doubtless intended as helpful advice,
this kind of thing is quite mischievous. Even if it is true
it is for the Synod to say what is competent for it and it
is certainly not for an inferior court to pass judgment
upon the extent of the Synod's powers.

The essential point to keep in mind is that what the
appellant is asking for here is not leave to appeal but
leave to have ten days in which to lodge his reasons of
appeal (see hereunder, page 132).

It would be proper at that same point—that is, when
judgment is intimated—that the dissatisfied member
of the Presbytery should make his dissent and
complaint. On the other hand he could quite properly
have done so before parties were recalled, at the time
when the Presbytery decision had been arrived at. It is
in order for other members of Presbytery if they so
desire to associate themselves with the dissent and
complaint, but not, of course, with the appeal. The
dissenting member has the same period of ten days'
grace in which to lodge the reasons for his complaint.

Challenging Procedure   The redress of dissent and
complaint, it should be added, is not confined to
"cases" where there is a party at the bar but is
available to any member of a Church court at any time
on any matter before the court, with a very limited set
of exceptions where the law of the Church stipulates
that finality of judgment is to lie with that particular
court. When it is desired to bring any decision under
review dissent should be taken immediately the
relevant decision has been reached. It may be that the

complaint has to do primarily with what is thought to be the irregularity of some particular step in the procedure, and in that event complaint should be made when the step is actually taken, and then made again at the end against the judgment reached. For example, you might argue that it was not in order to deal with this item of business at this meeting since no advance notice had been given. That point is discussed and a vote taken and you are defeated, or it may be that the Moderator rules without debate against you. In either event you then and there dissent and complain. In such circumstances the court will carry on with the business to the stage where it reaches a judgment upon it. At that point you dissent and complain once again— for if the procedure was wrong the conclusion is bound to be invalid. The court will not put its judgment into effect until either the dissent has been withdrawn or judgment has been given upon it in the superior court.

"Taking Instruments" The minute recording the fact of appeal traditionally reads, "... against which judgment Mr A. B. protested for leave to appeal, took instruments in the Clerk's hands, and craved extracts." This interesting phrase about taking instruments in the Clerk's hands covers the somewhat exciting ceremony of the appellant laying a shilling on the Clerk's table—to the interested delight, naturally, of the spectators, and to the no small embarrassment, normally, of the recipient. All of this is a survival from a time when litigation in the courts of the Church was very much the order of the day and the Presbytery Clerk, not being in receipt of any kind of regular salary, was wholly dependent for any income from the post on being paid so-much-a-page for extracts—which,

incidentally, had to be written out in long-hand. In order to process his appeal a litigant had to have extracts—so he craved them. And he had to pay for them—so as a token of his good faith in this respect he tabled his shilling. It was an earnest of his commitment to pay and it stands alongside the "arles" (the half-crown that used to be given to a farmhand on his being "waged" at a feeing-fair, or that was paid to the factor by the prospective tenant in a day when houses could be had to rent), and with the soldier's "shilling" paid to him on enlistment, voluntary or otherwise.

I am sure it's a pretty meaningless affair today, almost on a par with the coins people seem unable to resist throwing into fountains. A shilling is no longer legal currency, and the five-pence piece is of little help to any "pious purpose" to which the Clerk may donate it. I cannot imagine that the appeal would be in any way prejudiced were the transaction to be omitted. On the other hand members of Presbytery might feel that meetings are often dreich enough and that they should not be deprived of the occasional harmless diversion.

Lodging of Reasons   As indicated above, the party seeks leave to have ten days in which to lodge his reasons for appeal. The appeal itself has to be a subscribed writing containing its reasons. It would be unrealistic to expect that it could be produced at the meeting when the appeal is taken—hence the ten days' grace, which the court cannot refuse. It should be noted that in calculating the time limit the day when the appeal was taken is not counted as one of the ten. It is in order at any time to withdraw an appeal, and if this is to be done the fact should be intimated without needless delay. If the reasons are not lodged with the

Clerk within the prescribed period the appeal is assumed to have been departed from—and indeed cannot be revived.

From all of the foregoing it will be apparent that appeal and dissent and complaint are ways of bringing to a superior court for review some matter which has been regularly before, and has been judged upon by, some inferior court.

Petition

The normal use of petition is to initiate business in the court of first instance—the business usually having to do with the particular affairs of the petitioners. For example, the Society for the Prevention of Pornography might petition the Presbytery to have a document read from all pulpits when it was proposed to open a sex shop in the area; or somebody could petition to have made available for signatures at all services a paper that was ultimately to be forwarded to the Prime Minister; or it could be from the Society for the Protection of the Purity of Worship craving that ministers should be forbidden from having the Lord's Prayer sung in Church—or what have you. Or again it could be a petition from a Kirk Session asking the Presbytery to intervene in some dispute that had arisen within the congregation.

In this whole connection I think it should be said that Presbyteries have become much less formal in respect of their own affairs than once was the case and that today much of what ought properly to be the subject of petition is now achieved through a letter addressed to the Clerk and asking the help of the Presbytery in this or that. If what is being asked for is something which the Presbytery can grant only in its judicial capacity then I think it should require that the request take the appropriate form.

To be competent a petition must have a "crave"— that is to say, it should in so many words ask the Presbytery to take some specific action. Having set forth the significant facts briefly and succinctly under the heading, "The Petition of ... humbly sheweth that ..." it goes on, "May it therefore please your Reverend Court to do thus and thus", and it concludes, "or to do further or otherwise as in the premises may to your Reverend Court seem good." In this, it should be noted, it differs from an appeal which merely sets out the facts and which must not in any circumstances go on to suggest a course to be followed—at the risk of being treated as a petition.

In Place of Appeal   As well as this normal use of petition there is also a special use in the case where the petitioner should have proceeded by appeal or dissent and complaint but has been obstructed or otherwise prevented from following that course. Suppose, for example, in the instance I referred to earlier (page 130) that the Moderator had ruled an appeal would be incompetent and the Presbytery had refused to allow it or to grant extracts, then the would-be appellant could become a petitioner and reach the superior court along that avenue. I remember a case where the Kirk Session took disciplinary action against one of its elders in his absence and without his having been cited (on the odd argument that it was his duty to be at every meeting of Kirk Session and he must take the consequences if he absented himself). Had he been at the meeting he would, of course, have had to be called to the bar and when the case went against him and sentence was pronounced he would have appealed. In his absence from the meeting that course was obviously not available for him. He therefore brought the matter to the Presbytery by petition and was upheld in so doing. In such a case the petition should set forth the circumstances that have led to that method being resorted to in place of appeal as well as condescending on the merits of the case, and the propriety of having done this should be considered by the Presbytery when it resolves whether or not to receive the petition.

How Dealt With There are three stages in dealing with a petition when it comes before the Presbytery. First of all it has to be read (or taken as read), and unless it is quite obviously incompetent or offensive this will be agreed. Then it has to be received. Here again the test will be that of its competence, but it would be normal practice to hear the petitioner on the question of competence before resolving not to receive. And since it is always difficult to prove a negative it will be helpful if first some indication is given of the grounds on which it appears that competence could be challenged. And in the third place a decision has to be come to as to what answer will be made to its prayer. Before the Presbytery does this it will hear the petitioner on the merits, and he will be given an opportunity to answer questions from the floor of the Presbytery. If the answer to the prayer is to be in the negative then the petition may be "dismissed", but it cannot be dismissed until it has been received—any more than a servant can be dismissed before he has been engaged.

Having got to the Presbytery by way of petition the promoter is now in a position where, if his prayer is denied, he can proceed up the ladder of courts by way of appeal.

Reference

Should a Presbytery take the view that an issue before it raises questions of such serious importance and general concern that it would be desirable to have the mind of a higher court given to them, or should opinion in the Presbytery be seriously and fairly evenly divided upon a subject of some moment, it may resolve not to divide on the issue but to refer it *simpliciter* to a superior court. If that is to be done the court of first instance should not itself pass any judgment on the matter but simply resolve to refer. It is inviting the higher court to relieve it of the responsibility of judging, it is not asking it to confirm a judgment at which it itself has arrived. When the reference comes to the higher court the members of the referring court are not at the bar and are therefore free to vote on the issue.

Some years ago there came before the Presbytery a case which had achieved considerable publicity because it raised a very important and tricky question of doctrine. The Presbytery debated the matter at length, opposing motions were proposed and voted upon, and the votes were declared to be equal. The Moderator indicated that in his view it would be unfortunate if the case were to be decided upon his casting vote and that the matter might form the subject of a reference to the General Assembly. As I saw it this was a perfectly proper use of this particular instrument. But as I remember it the Procurator of that day opposed it on the ground that the particular matter in question was one where finality of judgment was given to the Presbytery and if the issue could not be appealed neither could it be referred. I am prepared to believe the advice was sound but I always think it's a pity when you allow yourself to be strangled in your own regulations.

Many years ago a case of considerable consequence was giving concern to one of the large Presbyteries. That body was quite overwhelmingly on one side, but there was reason to believe the matter would be appealed and go to the Assembly, and there were those who believed that opinion in the Assembly might be much more evenly divided. Someone had the brilliant idea that if the case were to go to the Assembly by reference the members of the Presbytery would be free to vote and the strong feeling within that court would be reflected in the result, whereas if it went by appeal the Presbytery would be at the bar and their votes would be lost. For tactical reasons, therefore, the matter was referred. This seems to me to be a quite wrong—if not actually a dishonest—use of reference. As I see it a reference should begin by stating clearly why resort is being had to this course, and if that argument is not convincing the matter should be sent back to the Presbytery with instruction that it itself should issue the case, leaving the Assembly free to fulfil its role as a court of appeal.

Today reference is principally invoked as a method of bringing to the judgment of the General Assembly cases where it has not been found possible to resolve disagreement between a Presbytery and an Assembly Committee on some issue where the concurrence of the latter body is necessary if the former body is to cause its judgment to become effective—usually a readjustment issue.

There, then, are the various avenues along which the review of a decision may be sought—the machinery of appeal in the courts of the Church.

Review by the Presbytery

We must now return from this long digression on the general pattern of review to a consideration of the immediate issue of the place of the Presbytery as a court of review. In this connection the Presbytery has to act as a court of appeal for those dissatisfied with decisions of Kirk Sessions, of Congregations, of Deacons' Courts, of Congregational Boards, and of Committees of Management. Let me take them one by one.

Kirk Session Decisions   With, I think, one solitary exception, a decision on any matter that has come before a Kirk Session can be made the subject of appeal or of dissent and complaint to the Presbytery of the bounds. The solitary exception is the decision of the Session on an application to be added to the List of Adherents on the Electoral Register that is prepared at the outset of a vacancy. Here it is specifically provided that the decision of the Kirk Session is final. A parishioner or member who has been disciplined by the Session may appeal from his place at the bar. On any issue that is before the court a member of Session may dissent and complain. The procedure is exactly as has been set out above for the case of appeal against a decision of Presbytery. A member of a congregation has always the right to approach the Presbytery by petition regarding any matter falling within the province of the Kirk Session.

Congregational Decisions   A member of a congregation who strongly disapproves of a decision reached at a congregational meeting (to sell the manse, for example) may dissent therefrom, and if he wishes to take the matter further he may approach the Presbytery which, in this case, he must do by petition. I remember an instance where at the congregational meeting at which the Vacancy Committee had been appointed it had been resolved that the election of the minister would be by ballot. By the time they had got to the stage of having chosen a sole nominee time was running out on them and they decided to cut a corner and have the election by open vote immediately after the nominee had preached. This they did and he was elected by a very large majority. A dissatisfied member petitioned the Presbytery to set aside the election on the ground of irregularity, and this the court had no alternative but to do. The ballot vote, I am happy to record, confirmed the heartiness of the choice. But the short-cut, as so often happens, turned out to be the long-way-round. I have often said I've lived long enough in the country to learn that the shortest distance between two points is not a straight line but the tar-macadam road that links them.

Deacons' Court Decision   The Act which in the former United Free Church dealt with the constitution and powers of the Deacons' Court stated clearly that "there is no right of regular appeal or complaint to the Kirk Session, or to any of the superior courts of the Church, against a decision of the Deacons' Court. Their determinations are final, when they keep within their province and obey the Acts of the General Assembly." The Act, however, went on to say, "Any member of a congregation, or of a Kirk Session, may petition the Presbytery against the procedure of the Deacons' Court on the ground of excess of power, or of disregard to Acts of Assembly." The situation then is that the Deacons' Court, so long as they stay rigidly within their powers and do not breach the law of the Kirk, are unassailable.

It should be noted that procedure, if review is being sought, is by petition. It is interesting that nothing should be said about the position of the individual deacon who considers a proposal of the court to be *ultra vires*. Presumably he should record his dissent as a deacon at the time of the meeting and then petition the Presbytery from his place as a member of the congregation.

If satisfied that there has been irregularity, the Presbytery has power to declare a judgment null and void and to order that the minute be expunged. The Deacons' Court has the right to appeal to the Synod against such a decision of the Presbytery.

Congregational Board Decisions   The Model Deed of Constitution for a Parish *quoad sacra* (1965) provides that "if any question shall arise with reference to the election of the Board, or to the interpretation of any Article of this Constitution, or to the legality of any particular exercise of the powers herein contained, it shall be competent to any person or body interested to apply by petition to the Presbytery to adjudicate upon the matter." Once again, it will be noted, the right of appeal is strictly limited to the regularity of procedure and not to the merits of decisions reached. And again the instrument of appeal is petition.

The Deed in this case, however, goes on to grant finality of judgment to the Presbytery on such a petition, with the exception that, if an aggrieved party can, within twenty-one days of the Presbytery decision, produce a certificate from the Procurator of the Church to the effect that the issue is one suitable for appeal to the Higher Courts, then an appeal or dissent and complaint may be proceeded with as though it had been regularly protested for at the time of the judgment. (This is the exception to the rule I referred to above (page 129) about appeal having to be taken immediately judgment is pronounced.)

Committee of Management Decisions I cannot find anywhere a direct reference to the matter of what remedy lies to the member of a former United Presbyterian congregation who is disgruntled about something in the conduct of the Committee of Management. But it seems to me there are two possibilities. The Committee of Management would readily agree, I think, that it is answerable to the congregation that elects it, so the dissatisfied member could raise his complaint at a congregational meeting called for temporal purposes. If he is successful the congregation would presumably instruct the Managers to take appropriate remedial action, while if he loses out at the meeting he can petition the Presbytery against a decision of a congregational meeting. Or again, every U.P. constitution contains a clause reserving "the constitutional right of the Kirk Session to watch over all the interests of the congregation, and to interpose whenever, in its opinion, the welfare of the congregation calls on it to do so, by convening meetings for any purpose connected with congregational affairs, or in any other competent manner." I take the view, therefore, that the member who felt the Managers had acted irregularly or *ultra vires* should in the first place seek the intervention of the Kirk Session to put things right. In the event that he was not satisfied with the answer he received from the Kirk Session he could then appeal and bring the matter to the Presbytery in the ordinary way. By following either of these routes he could reach the Presbytery— but in either case it would require two separate steps to get there.

7

Its Relation to Superior Courts

In this closing chapter I should like to look at the relationship of the Presbytery to the Synod and to the General Assembly. But before doing so I might say just a word about the Presbytery's relationship to other Presbyteries. The general principle is that a Presbytery cannot review or in any way interfere with the business of any other. Should a Presbytery feel aggrieved at some action or decision taken by another it may remonstrate on the subject, and, failing success along that line, it can bring the complaint to the Synod by petition if both Presbyteries are in the same Synod, otherwise to the General Assembly, also by petition.

It occasionally happens today in connection with readjustment that it would be desirable if a charge were to be transferred from the bounds of one Presbytery to those of another—so that it may be linked or united with a congregation there. Although both Presbyteries may be happy about the proposal it can be effected only by the Synod (or Assembly) on a petition asking the superior court to effect the change. Such petition should be at the instance of the receiving Presbytery and if possible it should have the concurrence of the other.

The Synod

Its Membership Until very recently the Synod consisted of all the members of the Presbyteries within its province. When a minister was entitled to or was granted a seat in Presbytery he was, in virtue of the same circumstances, the holder of a seat in Synod. Once a year Kirk Sessions met to appoint one of their number to represent them in Presbytery and Synod. An Act of 1981, while specifically reserving the right of any Synod to continue to be composed of all the members of its constituent Presbyteries as heretofore, provides that, with the concurrence of all its constituent Presbyteries, a Synod may resolve to confine its membership to a proportion only of its potential strength, the proportion to be determined by the Synod itself with approval of the General Assembly on a deliverance of the Board of Practice and Procedure, the choice of members to the number required to be made by the Presbyteries.

It is well known that for the past half-century the dwindling interest in Synods has been giving cause for concern. So much so that from time to time proposals have been advanced for the complete discontinuance of the Synod as a court of the Church. Attendances at the large Synods are generally very thin in relation to membership—the Synod of Clydesdale with a potential strength in the twelve hundred range is indeed well attended when there are 150 present—only an interesting "case" will bring that many. So the change has been made because it was felt that in the case of these large Synods the sheer numerical size militates against their being well supported, and that a minister or elder could be expected to feel a keener sense of responsibility towards a body to which he had been directly appointed. It remains to be seen how successful the change may prove. For myself I have long held the view that the Edinburgh committees now supply the intermediate stage between Presbytery and Assembly that used to be provided by the Synod and that therein lies the explanation of the dwindling interest and the falling attendances.

The main point to underline here is the constitutional change in the character of the Synod with the consequent duty now laid upon the Presbyteries of appointing those who are to constitute the superior court.

Presbytery Records   The Presbytery must annually submit to the Synod its minutes and its Benefice Register for inspection and attestation.

Quinquennial Visitation Reports   The Presbytery has to report to the Synod each year on the work of quinquennial visitation within its bounds, and in particular it has to draw attention to cases where it is unable to express satisfaction with the state of a congregation. In such an instance the Synod is required "to appoint a committee to make further visitation in conjunction with the Presbytery and to attempt to remedy what is deemed to be unsatisfactory." If matters are still amiss the fact is to be reported to the General Assembly through the General Administration Committee (now the Board of Practice and Procedure). One may be forgiven for remarking here again in passing that it is difficult to see how this much reporting and appointing of committees is going to help in the typical case where things are sore amiss and deep personality problems are at the root of the trouble.

Care of Property The 1970 Act provides that each Presbytery is annually to report to the Synod its diligence under the Act and that each Synod is to report to the General Assembly on the diligence of its constituent Presbyteries.

Recalling a Judgment It is, I think, generally accepted that in a Church court you cannot raise anew within a period of six months any matter on which it has already recorded a judgment. It is not so widely recognised that there are matters on which a court cannot of its own will recall its earlier judgment even after the expiry of the six month period. If the matter is something completely domestic to the Presbytery (its place of meeting, the size of its committees, its attitude to Sunday trading) then all is well. But if any second party has secured a right under the judgment it can be recalled only with that party's consent, or at the instance of a superior court. In a case in Auchterarder (not the famous one but a later affair in 1903) the Presbytery had changed its mind without consent of all possible parties and this the Sheriff characterised as "an incompetence apparent on the face of" their judgment. In circumstances like these the Presbytery should proceed by way of petition to the Synod, asking that court to recall the judgment, and it would then be the responsibility of the Synod to hear all parties who had an interest.

The General Assembly

Presbyteries appoint commissioners to the General Assembly, they may approach the Assembly by way of petition or overture, they have to provide the Assembly with an expression of opinion on all proposed new legislation. Let us look at each of these more fully.

Appointment of Commissioners

The Act of Union of 1929 ordained that the General Assembly should consist exclusively of commissioners (ministers and elders to the extent of a quarter of their membership) appointed by Presbyteries. An Act of 1956 broke with this tradition, providing that the Moderator, the Moderator-Elect, the Clerks, the Procurator, and the Law Agent should be members *ex officiis*. The year 1969 saw the addition of all ex-Moderators, but provided that they would come as commissioners from Presbyteries. Of late years there has been acceptance of an increasing number of Corresponding Members, in particular the Secretaries of the Standing Committees. Substantially, however, it is still true to say that the General Assembly consists of commissioners appointed by Presbyteries.

Use of Rota   The number of commissioners to which a Presbytery is entitled is one minister for every four or part thereof of the number of ministerial members on its Roll, and the same number of elders. Act XXIV of 1969 provided that, in addition to the above, a Presbytery could, if it so desired, return an ex-Moderator who was on its Roll, and that if it did so it was to appoint an extra elder so that parity might be maintained.

I imagine all Presbyteries operate some kind of rota whereby every minister gets an opportunity to attend at least once every four years, and whereby congregations get their turn of being invited to nominate an elder prepared to attend. In the latter connection it should be noted that such elders need not be members of Presbytery but that they attend the Assembly as commissioners from the Presbytery and not as representatives of their congregations. The Presbytery has to satisfy itself that every elder so appointed is a *bona fide* acting elder within its bounds.

It is important to note that a Presbytery is not obliged to observe any kind of rota and is free to appoint whom it will as its commissioners. Neither ministers nor congregations have any "rights" in the matter of commissioning to the General Assembly. Should at some time an issue arise that sharply divides the Church, creating strong feeling on each side, this point could become one of considerable concern—as it did in the period before the Disruption, the "Ten years' Conflict" of 1833–43. Examination of Presbytery records covering that period reveals the most heated wrangling, debating and voting over competing lists of proposed commissioners.

The Commission The actual terms of the commission are worthy of some attention. Messrs So-and-So are appointed "commissioners to the next General Assembly indicted to meet at Edinburgh on . . . , willing them to repair thereto, and to attend all the diets of the same, and there to consult, vote and determine in all matters that come before them, to the glory of God and the good of His Church, according to the Word of God, the Confession of Faith, and agreeable to the constitution of this Church, as they will be answerable; and that they report their diligence therein at their return therefrom." Clearly they are commissioners, not delegates. They cannot be instructed to vote in a particular way, so the only method for securing support for your cause is to ensure that only those are appointed who see things in what you regard as the proper light! Hence the competing lists of commissioners which, as I remarked above, enlivened many a Presbytery meeting in those bitter years. It could happen again.

An Act of 1877 required that commissioners be appointed in the two calendar months preceding that of the Assembly itself, and that the election follow upon a resolution to hold it taken not less than ten clear days previously. It is still required—though I do not think enforced—that the election take place "between the hours of eleven o'clock forenoon and eight o'clock in the evening."

If a commissioner withdraw another may be appointed in his place. And, strangely enough, if a minister be translated to a charge within a different Presbytery he can still represent the Presbytery which appointed him and take up the commission to the Assembly. This is true even if the translation had been agreed to before the election as a commissioner was made.

Diligence   The form of commission quoted above not only requires that the commissioner has to show diligence but also that he has to report it. I think that in all cases today it is presumed that those appointed have exhibited due diligence and the requirement to report the same is met by inviting one or more of the commissioners to report briefly at the first convenient Presbytery meeting on their impressions of the Assembly and of its business.

At the Bar   It is quite common for the Assembly to have to deal with a case where the activities of a particular Presbytery are brought under review. When that happens the commissioners from that Presbytery are "at the bar" and are not allowed to speak in the debate or to vote in the division. Should it be the Synod whose judgment is being challenged then that court will be at the bar and members of all its constituent Presbyteries are prevented from participation. The question has not yet arisen, but I am quite sure that this will hold even although under the new constitution of Synods not all of the Presbytery members are actually members of the court whose decision is being challenged. In practice there is always confusion when a Synod is involved. After all, you can scarcely wonder if an elder, not a member of Presbytery but representing it in the Assembly, does not know that he is also representing a Synod of whose existence he may never have heard. The confusion of many ministers is equally great—even if less easy to understand.

Frequently a case may reveal a strong difference of opinion between a Presbytery and a Committee of the General Assembly, and the latter may seem to be every bit as much a "party" in the affair as is the former. An Assembly Committee, however, does not go to the bar—this would be tantamout to having the Assembly at its own bar—so that the members of the Committee are at liberty to take their full part in determining the outcome of the case—as they often do. This is perfectly regular, but I always feel that it is most unfortunate, for it can so easily give the impression that justice is not being done. If it is at all possible I feel that such cases should be brought under reference (see above, page 136 ff), as this does not involve either side being at the bar.

In the interesting case mentioned a couple of paragraphs earlier where a minister has been translated since his election as a commissioner, such a man would be free, as I see it, to vote on an issue in which his new Presbytery was at the bar so long as the

Presbytery whose commission he held was not involved. Whether he would be well advised so to do is quite another matter.

Petition and Overture

There are two ways in either of which a Presbytery may elect to approach the General Assembly—petition and overture. (This, of course, in addition to the ways in which a Presbytery may be brought before the Assembly when one of its judgments is challenged.) The distinction between these two is that overture is employed to raise in the Assembly some matter of general interest and concern to the Kirk whereas the role of petition is to initiate an item of business of particular and private interest to the Presbytery. For instance, if the Presbytery were anxious that the Assembly should appoint a committee to examine and report on the incidence of drug addiction among young people, it would do so by promoting an overture; if the Presbytery were anxious to have its boundaries with a neighbouring Presbytery adjusted it would approach the Assembly by petition.

Procedurally the principal difference is that a petition is sent direct to the Assembly whereas in the case of an overture this has to be transmitted by the Synod. The Synod has no power to refuse to transmit an overture that is in proper form no matter how hostile it may be to the substance of it. It has, however, the right to transmit with Approval or with Disapproval, and it may also transmit *cum nota,* the note being a comment either of commendation or of suggested amendment. In the case where no meeting of Synod intervenes, a Presbytery may send its overture direct to the Assembly.

In form, as has been explained above (page 134), a Petition begins by "humbly shewing" the various circumstances of the case and goes on to crave the Assembly to take some specific step, adding the proviso that the Assembly may "do further or otherwise as to your Venerable Court may seem good", and it concludes with the respectful assurance, "and your petitioners will ever pray." An overture, on the other hand, sets forth its condescendences in a series of paragraphs beginning, "Whereas ... And whereas ... And whereas ..." and it concludes by "humbly overturing" the General Assembly to take some step. Of recent years I have noted a tendency to add the bit about "doing further or otherwise" but for my own part I do not believe that this properly belongs to an overture.

A petition will normally have the effect of taking the petitioning Presbytery to the bar of the Assembly. An overture leaves the members of the Presbytery free to participate in debate and in division. Although in theory an overture emanates from a Presbytery, in fact it is normally the result of the efforts of an individual within the Presbytery. An individual who has a matter he wants aired in the Assembly can conveniently get there only by persuading his Presbytery to overture. Not unnaturally, therefore, it is usual for the presentation to be entrusted to the person who has been the moving spirit behind it. If a commissioner, he presents it from the rostrum; if not a commissioner, he presents it from the bar.

Assembly Remits

It is not unusual today for a proposal which has been before the Assembly to be sent down by that body to

Presbyteries for consideration and comment. This is a most valuable way both for discovering the mind of the Church on the merits of the proposal and for polishing up the minutiae of any necessary legislation. It can be counted upon to produce much more constructive comment and detailed criticism than will be forthcoming in course of any Assembly debate, no matter how inspired or inspiring that debate may be or how much time may have been devoted to it.

Overtures under the Barrier Act

Before any new legislation can be approved by the General Assembly it has to "go down to Presbyteries under the Barrier Act" and it must receive the approval of not less than half of the Presbyteries of the Church if the following Assembly is to convert it into an Act.

The Barrier Act became law in 1697 when the Kirk was under fairly heavy pressure and there was a danger of General Assemblies succumbing to panic and being rushed into acceptance of ill-considered legislation. It was the purpose of the Act to prevent this. It provides that before the Assembly can pass any Acts which are to be "binding rules and constitutions to the Church" these must be proposed by way of overture to the Assembly, and, if approved (by that Assembly) are to be remitted to Presbyteries for consideration and for report to the next General Assembly which may convert the overture into an Act "if the more general opinion of the Church thus had agreed thereto."

Interim Act Imagine, then, that a proposal comes to the Assembly to amend legislation affecting doctrine, government, worship or discipline within the Church—to allow a new class of person a seat in

Presbytery, for example—then the Assembly can vote against the proposal and that is the end of the matter. If, however, the Assembly approve, the most they can do is to adopt the overture and agree that it be sent down to Presbyteries under the Barrier Act. They can, in fact, go further and pass an Interim Act making the legislation effective immediately but subject to the restriction that it may have to be rescinded the following year should the necessary Presbytery support not be forthcoming. Obviously, therefore, such an Interim Act is likely to be passed only when there is some urgency and the matter has been unanimously approved at Assembly and there seems no possibility of opposition arising. In the case I instanced above it would be most unfortunate to grant seats in Presbytery to a group of people and next year to have to withdraw from that position. So the Interim Act has a limited usefulness.

At Presbytery The Presbytery has to appoint and give advance notice of the meeting at which the Barrier Act remit will be considered. The Overture is to be put to the Presbytery in the simple form, Approve or Disapprove, a vote has to be taken and the precise numbers voting recorded (even when the vote is unanimous). It is in order also for the Presbytery to transmit a Note in regard to the Overture. It must, at the same time, be recognised that no such Note can have any effect on the fate of the Overture and that it is therefore of comparatively limited value. What in effect the Presbytery might be regarded as saying is, "Had the overture instead of saying This-and-this said That-and-that we should have approved of it more heartily or we should have approved instead of disapproving of it." It is true that this may be of considerable value to the promoting body which may wish, if the overture is defeated, to advance it in an amended form at some later date. But that is about the extent of the worth of a Note appended to a Barrier Act return. For my own part I think we should be better off without the possibility of the Note—Presbyteries would see more vividly the stark choice, "Do you want precisely what has come down, or don't you?"

It is in order for a Presbytery to direct attention in a Note to what is in effect an error or omission in the Overture. Where suggested changes of this kind "in no way modify the substance, sense or intention of the overture, it is competent for the General Assembly, if they see cause, to adopt the substance of them."

In the year 1979 some matters that had been sent down under the Barrier Act inspired an enormous wealth of comment. In particular there were three overtures—the Act anent the Auxiliary Ministry, an Act anent Membership of Presbytery, and the Act setting up the Assembly Council—which produced respectively nine, five, and eight pages of comments as printed in the Blue Book for 1980. To me this is a nonsense. It shows clearly that these Acts were not ripe for Barrier Act treatment but that they should instead have been sent down for consideration and comment. Since this had not been done they should, in my opinion, have been withdrawn at the Assembly and taken back for further consideration and adjustment in the light of the many very helpful comments received. They could then have become Barrier Act overtures the following year. The question which the Barrier Act presents is not, "Do you think something along these general lines would be desirable?" The question is quite starkly, "Do you want this Act precisely as it stands—warts and all—to become part of the law of the Church?" If the answer is not an unequivocal "Yes" then it must be an emphatic "No". Good legislation is far more important than instant legislation.

"The More General Opinion" The Act speaks about "the more general opinion of the Church". This has been interpreted as meaning a majority of the Presbyteries of the Church irrespective of how many may have returned a vote and without regard to what may have been the state of the voting in each of them. At present there are 48 Presbyteries with a right to Barrier Act vote and it is essential if an overture is to survive that it shall have been approved by 25 Presbyteries. Suppose, for example, that 23 Presbyteries approved, 3 disapproved, and the others made no return, the overture would fall. The relative size of the Presbyteries and the number voting therein are irrelevant considerations. A "Disapprove" arrived at on the casting vote of the Moderator at Uist (28 members) has identical value with a unanimous "Approve" in Glasgow (approximately 600 members). The degree of injustice which this might seem to indicate is, I think, more apparent than real. I am not aware of a single case where a different result would have emerged had the number of votes been the deciding factor instead of the number of Presbyteries. Occasionally, it is true that what "just made it" on Presbyteries would have romped home on votes, and, at the opposite extreme, there has been the odd case where the majority of Presbyteries in favour has been in a proportion of roughly ten to one while the number of votes has been roughly five to three.

The Last Word A further point of some interest is

that the last word still lies with the General Assembly. Let it be that the Assembly of 1976 approved the Overture and sent it down, let it be that a clear majority of Presbyteries voted for approval, the Assembly of 1977 is still free to pass or not to pass as in its wisdom it sees fit. This was exemplified some years ago in what some regard as a very startling fashion when a proposal regarding a change affecting the Church's relation to its subordinate standard was rejected by the Assembly although it had secured what was in that case the necessary two-thirds majority of the Presbyteries, and that in two consecutive years. I see the point as a most important one constitutionally in that it secures the position of the General Assembly—and not of the Presbyteries—as the supreme court of the Church. It is in the General Assembly that the last word is to be spoken.

The Barrier Act confers upon Presbyteries a power of veto to restrict the activity of the General Assembly; it does not put them in a position where they can direct or compel the General Assembly to take action.

The Articles Declaratory

A highly specialised form of Barrier Act procedure applies in the case where it is proposed that some change should be made in the Articles Declaratory. It is not within the scope of this work—even if it were within the competence of the writer—to enter into a discussion in any detail of what exactly these Articles constitutionally speaking are, of what is the nature of the Church's relation to them, or of the effects that might follow upon changes made in them. Suffice it to say that the Articles Declaratory of the Constitution of the Church of Scotland in Matters Spiritual represents a document prepared in the first instance by the Church of Scotland in anticipation of union with the United Free Church, that it was approved by both of these Churches at Assembly and Presbytery levels, that it was approved by both Houses of Parliament, and that it received the Royal Assent on 28th July 1921, though its provisions were not brought into force until five years later.

I could not possibly hope to express better what Cox has to say about the constitution of the Kirk, so I quote at length—"The constitution of the Church of Scotland is, if not wholly at least to a large extent, set forth in certain documents to which it is bound within limits to adhere. Though as a Divine institution it must remain free to follow the guidance of the Spirit of God, as He interprets from one generation to another the Holy Scriptures, which form at once its royal charter and its supreme standard, from which there can be no deviation, yet as a human institution the Church requires a clear and authoritative statement of its principles and definite rules, according to which the affairs of the Church are to be transacted, that there may be neither injustice nor confusion. These principles and rules, framed as they have been in successive ages in accordance with the necessities of the time in the light of experience gained in the past, yet always liable to be modified by vision of future developments, may in their totality be said to form the Constitution of the Church of Scotland as we know it in our own day."

The Articles Declaratory represent what is certainly the most important instrument of the constitution, and clearly any proposal to alter these Articles is a matter of the most grave concern.

The first of the Nine Articles sets forth the basic doctrinal position of the Church, and adherence to this, as it is interpreted by the Church, is declared to be essential to the Church's continuity and corporate life. It is further declared that the other Articles may be modified or added to provided the following procedure is observed. The Overture proposing the change has to be approved by the General Assembly and is then to be sent down to Presbyteries under the Barrier Act. In this case Presbyteries are to be free to make comments and suggestions, but are also to indicate approval or otherwise. If the Overture shall have received the approval of at least two-thirds of the Presbyteries of the Church it may then be modified if thought wise in the light of the Presbytery comments, and the finished product is then to be sent down once more. On this occasion Presbyteries are merely to indicate whether or not they approve. Again if more than two-thirds of the Presbyteries of the Church approve the matter is to be reported to the next Assembly which "may, if it deems it expedient, modify and add to these Articles in terms of the said Overture."

If the Overture fail, the same or a similar overture is not to be sent down again till after an interval of at least five years.

Conclusion

I began this little work with a comment upon the importance that has come over the years to attach to the Presbytery as a court of the Church. It is, then, perhaps fitting to conclude it by drawing attention to what has been said immediately above about the fact that while Presbyteries have a considerable say-so in determining the legislation—and even the constitution—of the Church, the General Assembly still holds its place of supremacy at the pinnacle of the pyramid.

Glossary

ab officio—from office

ad hoc committee—a committee set up for that purpose and no other

ad vitam aut culpam—for life or until fault

alibi—contention that the person was elsewhere at the specific time

bar, the—place occupied by parties appearing before the court

benefice—the provision for the living for a minister

bona fide—in good faith

competent—permissible in law

congé d'élire—the right to choose (a minister)

cum nota—accompanied by a comment

de die in diem—from day to day

ex gratia—from favour (as opposed to of right)

ex officio—in virtue of the office held

fama—a scandalous report

fama clamosa—a *fama* that has gained very wide circulation

heresy—an opinion at variance with the official standard of the Church

in hunc effectum—for that purpose and that alone

in retentis—papers not recorded but preserved

instanter—immediately, on the spot

ipso facto—by the very fact itself

ius devolutum—a right of which someone is deprived because he has not exercised it timeously

listed expenses—six expenses payable to ministers in addition to stipend

locum tenens—a person holding an office temporarily

locus standi—right to appear before a court

modus operandi—way of working

oath *de fidele (administratione officii)*—an undertaking faithfully to undertake the duties of an office

onus probandi—the responsibility for producing proof

preses—the chairman of the Board of Managers (ex U.P.)

prima facie—on the face of things

privilege—protection from penalty for what might otherwise be actionable as defamatory because made in course of public duty

Procurator—an official of the General Assembly, a senior counsel, who advises on legal matters, particularly in the civil field

pro re nata—for a matter that has arisen

pro tempore—for the time being

quoad sacra—in respect of sacred things

quorum—the minimum number whose attendance will constitute a meeting of a court

rubric—heading entered in the margin of a minute-book

sederunt—those present

simpliciter—without comment

sine die—without a time-limit being specified

teind—a tax on the fruit of the land for the support of religious ordinances

translation—the movement of a minister from one parish to another

ultra vires—beyond the legitimate power of the court

victual stipend—stipend paid in quantities of actual grain (prior to 1808)

Index